WORLD WAR II
SMALL ARMS

WORLD WAR II
SMALL ARMS

John Weeks

BLACK CAT

Endpapers: British troops, armed with a Bren gun and Lee-Enfield rifles, help guard the Maginot Line before the fall of France in 1940.

Title page: US troops wade ashore with Garand M1 rifles during the Pacific campaign.

Below: Italian troops take part in a training exercise shortly before the outbreak of war.

Page 6: Men of the Afrika Korps prepare their machine gun for action during the North African campaign.

© Copyright Orbis Publishing Ltd 1979
© Copyright Macdonald & Co (Publishers) Ltd 1988

First published 1979 in Great Britain by Orbis Publishing Ltd, London
Reprinted 1988 by Macdonald & Co (Publishers) Ltd under the Black Cat imprint
Macdonald & Co (Publishers) Ltd
3rd Floor
Greater London House
Hampstead Road
London NW1 7QX
a member of Maxwell Pergamon Publishing Corporation plc

ISBN 0-7481-0111-X

Printed in Singapore by Kim Hup Lee
Printing Co Pte Ltd

Picture Acknowledgements

Imperial War Museum/Orbis: Endpapers, 13, 16–17, 29b, 72–73, 75, 77, 81, 82, 86–87, 92–93, 104–105, 131, 138
US Marine Corps/Orbis: Title Page, 11, 128–129, 132
Orbis: 8–9
IWM/Robert Hunt Library: 10, 38, 78–79b, 102–103
Bundesarchiv/RHL: 18–19, 28
Armeria Eugenio Sacchi, Milano/Istituto Geografico de Agostini, Novara: 20, 76
Raccolta ditta Armi Jäger, Milano/IGDA: 21, 22b, 46, 46–47t, 124
RHL: 22t, 35b, 58, 66–67, 112, 125t
Museo Storico Italiano della Guerra, Rovereto/IGDA: 24l, 24r, 26–27t, 26–27b, 30l, 30r, 35t, 37, 46–47, 47, 52, 52–53, 62, 75t, 83, 84–85, 87, 96–97, 102, 116t, 117, 118, 128–129, 130–131
Orbis: 25
John Weeks: 28l, 29t, 32, 39, 40, 40–41, 54–55, 56–57, 60, 61, 64–65t, 64–65b, 68–69, 69, 70–71, 74, 78–79t, 80–81, 88–89, 90–91, 94–95, 98, 99, 100–101, 106, 108–109t, 108–109b, 114–115, 118–119, 120, 120–121, 125b, 126, 137, 138–139, 140–141
SADO/RHL: 32–33
RHL: 36
Museo Nazionale d'Artiglieria, Torino/IGDA: 34, 94, 132–133, 134–135
Bibliotheque Nationale/IGDA: 42–43
Museo della Pusterla di Sant' Ambroglio, Milano/IGDA: 44
Signal/Orbis: 45l
Fabbricca d'Armi Beretta/IGDA: 45r
Raccolta P. Beretta/IGDA: 48–49t, 48–49b
Signal/IGDA: 51
Keystone/Orbis: 63, 140t
Fox Photos/Orbis: 88
ECP Armées/RHL: 101
Museo degli Alpini, Trento/IGDA: 107, 110–111, 112–113
Novosti/Orbis: 109, 113, 114, 116b
Masami Tokoi/Orbis: 121
US Marine Corps/RHL: 122–123, 136–137, 140b
D. Lubin/Orbis: 126–127

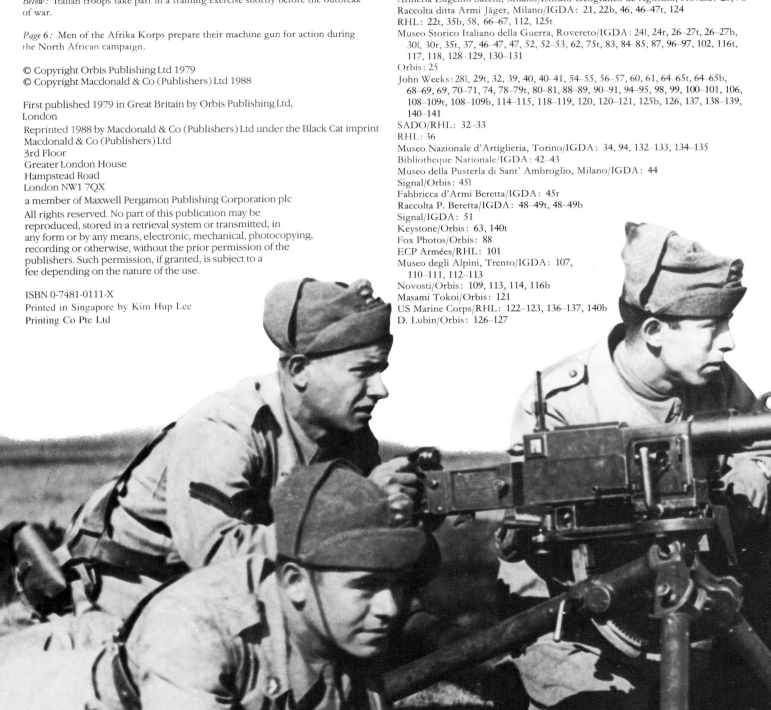

Contents

Foreword

by Brigadier Peter Young, DSO, MC, MA, FSA.

Success in war depends upon numerous factors; questions of politics, strategy and logistics all affect the outcome. But when it comes to combat on the actual battlefield it is tactics that count. There, the two main factors are the use of ground and of weapons. Without a thorough knowledge of weapons and their characteristics the modern soldier can look for little success in battle.

The armies of 1939 went to war, broadly speaking, with the small arms of 1918. The Germans, it is true, had adopted the submachine gun, and the British were replacing the Lewis gun, with its multitudinous stoppages, with the robust and reliable Bren. But weapons development had been neglected in the 20 years following 'the War to end Wars'. It may be that this very neglect caused the Second World War to be, as the author says, 'a period of unusually prolific advances in weapon design'.

The soldier who has to fight the battle wants weapons that have a good range and rate of fire, are accurate, are light to carry, robust and easy to maintain. It should not be beyond the wit of man, one might think, to achieve these aims. Not the least fascinating part of this book is the light it sheds on the way that parsimonious governments and conservative war ministries managed to send their troops forth to the Second World War with weapons already obsolescent in 1918. The French, for example, had the Lebel rifle – which had been 'the latest thing in infantry weaponry in 1886'!

It is interesting to see that the Germans, whose military skill is so much admired, were also capable of making mistakes. The production of the Model 98 Karabiner is a case in point. Having been missed by numerous German riflemen between 1940 and 1944, I have often wondered why the Germans, so skilful with mortar and light machine gun, were such rotten shots with the rifle. Well, now I know: 'Unfortunately,' the author writes (without considering my feelings!), 'it was a relatively awkward rifle to shoot, and the bolt action was most disappointing. The sight radius was short, which did not make for good shooting.' In No. 3 Commando, which I commanded in Italy and Normandy, we were always glad to acquire Lugers or 'Schmeissers', and sometimes used the MG 34. Nobody ever bothered to keep a German rifle. The firepower of the platoon is a decisive factor in infantry combat, and by giving their men a rifle that was so much less effective than the Garand, or even the old Lee-Enfield, the Germans were making life unnecessarily difficult for themselves at section level.

This is a fascinating book by a real expert, and simply packed with information. To the men who carted these weapons around in World War II it will be a real eye-opener, but it will appeal to the far wider circle of military historians, collectors of militaria, and war-gamers who still keep up the interest in our warlike heritage.

Peter Young

Introduction

The dictionary defines a small arm as 'a weapon that can be carried by hand, e.g. pistols, revolvers, shot-guns, rifles, etc', and this fairly sweeping classification is usually enough for most purposes. There are other ones, generally ones which try to define the limits of what can reasonably be called a hand-carried weapon, and it is now popular to specify a maximum calibre for small arms and refer to any bigger weapons as cannon or automatic cannon. For this study we will avoid such complications and stick to the simplest possible grouping, considering small arms as the dictionary describes them – weapons which can be carried by hand – though from time to time it will be seen that more than one hand needs to be used in the carrying process.

Small arms are the basic weapons of any army, for all soldiers are given a rifle in their basic training and taught to shoot with it. They may afterwards become artillerymen or tank drivers, but the initial skill is impressed on them all and in extreme emergency they are expected to be able to use it. For the infantry, small arms are the very basis of their existence. Despite the introduction of all the miscellany of modern infantry weapons – mortars, grenades, rocket launchers and the rest – it is still the rifle and bayonet of the infantryman which ultimately carries the day and forces the enemy to surrender. Never was this more clearly seen than in the recent jungle fighting in Vietnam.

The Second World War was a period of unusually prolific advances in weapon design, including small arms, and such

a period may never recur. Weapons are now too expensive, large and complicated to ever be treated with the same degree of experiment as they were between 1939 and 1945. That war started with most infantry carrying much the same simple equipment as had been used by their fathers 20 years before in World War I, but by the end the changes had been profound: there were few whose technical skills were restricted to just the simple rifle and bayonet, and there was now a whole range of infantry weaponry to be mastered and used. It is for this reason that the war is attractive to

Below: US troops, holding a wide selection of small arms, display the trophies they have captured from the Japanese after jungle fighting on a Pacific island.

the student of small arms, for the development of different systems can be easily followed since it is compressed into such a short time-scale. It will no doubt help the general reader if we briefly review the sort of changes that appeared, and which will be dealt with in this book.

One of the more remarkable innovations was the appearance of the submachine gun. From being an obscure curiosity in 1918 and a despised 'Gangster Gun' in the 1930s, the submachine gun broke through to become a major weapon by the middle of the war. It was helped by alarmist propaganda

years. Despite such a start in life, it now looks as if the submachine gun is reaching the end of its career and is being ousted by the lightweight high-powered rifle, which can offer a greater fire effect for the same weight. But in its day the submachine gun was supreme.

World War II also saw the introduction of self-loading rifles on a large scale. The US Army actually started with a self-loader, the Garand, and kept it in service throughout, manufacturing about 4.2 million by 1945. Other countries experimented and used a variety of designs, mainly in small

Above: Winston Churchill examines one of the first Thompson submachine guns to be sent to Britain.

stemming from the German paratroops, who carried it in substantial numbers, and from the realization that cheap firepower on a large scale was what often wins battles. The submachine gun gave the individual infantryman a huge improvement in his close-range effectiveness and it formed the ideal complement to the high-powered rifle. It was easy to make, light to carry, simple to operate and only suffered from a lack of range and occasional stoppages. Most types could fire the ammunition used by the other side, which was a useful feature shared by few other weapons. The manufacture of submachine guns became a major industry by the end of the war, and probably 10,000,000 were made altogether, many if not most of which survived into the post-war

numbers for special troops, but the majority of infantrymen carried bolt-action rifles of one kind or another from 1939 to 1945, and it was not until the mid-1950s that the self-loading rifle became universal. The Germans brought out the assault rifle, to use a modern term, though only in small numbers, but despite the modest beginning this was the start of the modern rifle design trend, and it stemmed from another German idea, the medium-powered cartridge.

The medium-powered cartridge was no new idea; it had been realized for many years, certainly since 1917, that the

10

usual rifle cartridge was far too powerful for most purposes, and required a larger and heavier rifle than was needed. But the economics of cartridge-making and the huge stocks of ammunition held by all countries made it very difficult to change, and no government was going to attempt it in peace-time. Germany, once again the initiator, designed a cut-down 7.92mm cartridge, and used it in the range of assault rifles designed in the early years of the war. This medium cartridge allowed a radical change in the weapon design and gave the rifleman a truly versatile weapon, but once again economics defeated the full realization of the system, and only a small proportion of the German output of small-arms ammunition was changed over. Ironically, it was the Soviets who benefited most, for they copied some captured rounds, adapted an existing design to fire it, developed the resulting weapon further, and the final product was the notorious Kalashnikov AK 47 of 1947, the weapon of every revolutionary movement in the world today.

Allied to the assault rifles and submachine gun designs was a fundamental change of manufacturing philosophy, stemming from the need to make vast quantities of small arms in a very short time. Until the 1930s, and often afterwards in some cases, small arms were made by traditional methods employing much machining of solid metal blocks, careful hand-fitting, and finely set tolerances on moving parts. For submachine guns this was impossibly expensive, and the methods of the automobile industry were brought in. Sheet-metal pressings replaced expensive forgings, plastic replaced walnut, tolerances were opened up. It worked perfectly well, and assault rifles were made in the same way. By using these methods the different parts of one weapon could be spread out among several factories, and only brought together for final assembly. Here again Germany gave the lead (though Soviet Russia followed quickly enough), and despite continuous Allied bombing of the known arms centres in Germany, the production of the simpler weapons was never seriously held up.

Another feature of the war was the anti-tank rifle. The first ones were used in 1917 by Germany, and their success prompted a whole range of them among continental armies by 1939. Not many were ever used in action; by 1941 they were all out of date because tank armour had outstripped their rather feeble ammunition, and by 1945 all but a few in the Soviet armies had vanished altogether. Theirs was a short life, and not a very effective one, but they offer an intriguing study and the ingenuity of the designers was remarkable. We shall be examining a few in the following chapters, though some of them are scarcely describable as small arms in the general sense of the term.

Coupled with changes in design were changes in the use of the weapons. Before the war it was traditional to regard the rifleman as the mainstay of the infantry. World War I had been fought with waves of bayonet-carrying infantry assaulting trench lines, supported by artillery barrages. The idea of the omnipotence of the rifleman had not entirely died

out in 1939, despite the proven ability of the defensive machine gun to defeat him. But in the German Army each squad had a machine gun, and the task of the squad was to keep that gun in action. The riflemen were secondary to the machine gun, which was rightly seen as the firepower of the whole team. Britain thought rather differently, and though giving the squad a gun, it was lighter and was not at first looked upon as the lynchpin of the squad. Battle experience changed that view. In the USA it was thought that the Garand could do away with the need for a machine gun

Above: A machine-gun crew covers an advance of US Marines on Saipan with their water-cooled Browning.

altogether, though this was soon modified and the Browning Automatic Rifle was used to back up the riflemen. Proof came in the drawn-out slogging battles in Russia, the Pacific and Italy. It was soon seen that what counted more than anything else was firepower and in practical warfare the machine gun replaced the rifle as the prime infantry weapon. Bayonets were hardly ever used except to shepherd prisoners.

In the following chapters we shall be following the story of each individual nation and its small arms in World War II. The subject is vast and can become hopelessly complicated, but the intention is to approach it in as simple a way as possible, explaining the reasons for each aspect. Not every weapon can be covered, and some may quarrel with the choice, but the criterion has had to be that of common use. A few unusual ones have been inserted because they are of particular interest, either from a design standpoint, or because of some effect they had upon military thinking. Because some technicalities are inevitable in such a work, the next chapter sets out to explain the principles of operation of small arms to those who may be unfamiliar with them. The expert can skip it if he wishes without losing anything of the main thread of the book; those less conversant with the internals of rifles and machine guns may find it helpful.

The Workings of Small Arms

All the small arms described in this book have similar general features. For all, the ammunition is composed of two parts – the cartridge case and the bullet. The case is generally made of brass, though there are some steel ones, and it performs several functions. Firstly it contains the propellant, and protects it from damp and damage. Secondly it carries the means of ignition in its base, and we shall only be dealing with one means of ignition – a simple cap or primer which is struck by a pin or hammer. Thirdly it holds the bullet and loads it at the same time as the propellant. Finally it acts as a seal to the rear end of the breech. When the cartridge is fired, the case expands and fills up the tiny spaces left around the edges of the breech, keeping in the high-pressure gas. This then is the basic cartridge, made in all sizes in unbelievable quantities by highly automated methods.

When one of these cartridges is fired, the propellant burns very quickly; in most cases all of it is consumed within one or two thousandths of a second, and it produces a large volume of hot gas. The gas is about 14,000 times greater in volume than the unburnt material, and this naturally gives rise to an enormous pressure within the case. In fact, the pressure in a rifle cartridge is about 20 tons per square inch and it acts upon the walls of the case, the base of the bullet, and the base of the case. This huge pressure gives the bullet its tremendous acceleration, and the hot gas follows it up the barrel to the muzzle. At the muzzle it expands with a bang, giving the characteristic noise of a small arm, and also producing a flash. As the bullet moves up the barrel, the weapon starts to recoil. This is because the case is given the same push backwards as the bullet is given forwards. A light, slow-moving bullet gives little recoil; a heavy, fast-moving one gives plenty. It is the bullet and its speed which determine recoil, and no amount of springs or buffers will get rid of it; all that they do is to reduce the shock to the firer. But recoil can be useful, as we shall see.

In the basic gun diagram on page 14 the main item is the barrel. The barrel is grooved internally with a spiral to spin the bullet as it moves up, and so give it gyroscopic stability in flight. The length of the barrel is designed to allow all the powder to burn out and give the bullet the maximum amount of push, for too short a barrel will allow gas to waste itself at the muzzle and give a large flash and explosion. The rear end of the barrel is opened out into a breech or chamber in which the cartridge is loaded. This chamber is then closed by a breech block or bolt, which has a striker in it. In this basic gun the breech block is firmly locked to the barrel, and so when the round is fired the pressure on the breech block pulls the gun backwards and gives the recoil force.

There are many ways of locking the breech, but the most common are the following three. The first and most usual lock is by a rotating bolt. This bolt has lugs on it and they engage with recesses on the body or breech; the bolt is pushed home to the breech face and turned to lock the lugs into the recesses. It is a method that is simple, reliable and strong. The second method is by some form of prop or strut. The breech block is held against the face of the breech by a strut which is hinged to it and is opened out to lock in front of a lug. This is also a simple method in outline, but there is a wide variety of types of strut and methods of operating them. Finally there is the family of locks which use a tilting block. With these the entire breech block is used as the strut, and when it has reached the breech face it is tilted to one side (or up or down) so that its rear edge drops into a recess in the body. Here again there is much ingenuity and invention in the methods of achieving the locking and unlocking.

Turning now to what a small arm has to do to discharge its bullet, we find that there is a whole series of mechanical operations which break down in the following way. On firing, the breech has to remain locked until the pressure has dropped to a safe level; the breech then has to be *unlocked.* After that the empty case has to be *extracted,* i.e. pulled out. It then has to be *ejected* clear of the mechanism and a fresh round picked up and *fed* to the breech and *chambered.* The breech is then *locked* by the breech block or bolt, which has contrived to *recock* the striker while moving. Finally the round is *fired.* In simple hand-operated rifles these actions are done by the firer opening and closing the bolt. In a revolver the hammer and trigger do the work, using the firer's fingers to provide the motive power. But in machine guns and all other automatic weapons the cycle of operations is achieved using the power of the propellant in each cartridge case. The designer has no easy task in using the impulsive blow of the propellant to work all these operations with the smallest and lightest mechanism possible, while also ensuring that they are tough enough to stand up to the enormous accelerations and pressures without failing or giving trouble. Most armies demand that the materials used should be the cheapest possible, that as little machining as possible should be involved, and that all parts should be interchangeable.

Some designs are complicated, some simple. Some work well, others gave continual trouble. Some are elegant and attractive to look at, some are downright ugly. It is this wide spread of mechanical ingenuity that makes the study of small arms so compelling and appealing. Nothing else approaches it for variety and diversity, and although it may be thought that in this book we shall be examining a major part of the

Right: The submachine gun greatly increased in popularity during the war. Here, British troops train with the military version of the US Thompson.

field, the range of all systems is far wider than just those of World War II, and the number is still increasing today.

But the main complication comes in the automatic weapons, and these used three systems for their basis of operation in World War II – *gas, recoil* and *blowback*. Some used two or more; none, so far as we know, used all three. The *recoil* system is the oldest of all, and the most obvious one to try first. With this the locked barrel and breech are allowed to move backwards under the recoil force as one unit. Their combined mass is sufficient to ensure that they do not move much more than about ½in (12.5mm) before the bullet has left the muzzle and the pressure has fallen. The barrel then stops and the bolt moves on under its own momentum, having unlocked itself. On the backward journey it extracts and ejects the cartridge case, and having reached the limit of travel, it moves forward again under the influence of the return spring, and feeds another round into the chamber on the way. The barrel is usually returned to its firing position by its own spring, but in a few designs the bolt helps too.

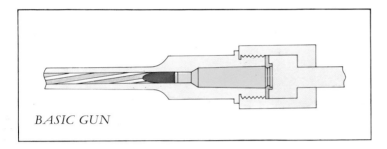

BASIC GUN

This principle is used in a great many machine guns and automatic pistols; it is reliable, robust, suffers little from fouling troubles and offers a simple barrel change. On the other hand it is rather heavy for a rifle and has no easy means of adjusting the amount of power. Strangely enough, it is not particularly powerful anyway, and most machine guns have had to fit recoil boosters to get sufficient energy to work their mechanisms. The booster is a chamber at the muzzle which traps some gas and allows it to expand and push on a flange attached to the muzzle.

The disadvantage of recoil operation is that it usually is heavier than any other system, and the barrel has to be able to move to and fro. But it needs fewer parts than the others, and this gives it reliability, which is essential in a machine gun.

The next system is gas operation, in which a small quantity of gas is tapped off from the barrel and used to drive a piston. The tapping hole is at least half-way up the bore, and so the bullet is already well on its way when it passes it; the small amount of gas taken off makes no difference to the bullet. This gas is turned round and directed back towards the breech, and shortly after turning it meets a piston and pushes on it. This piston is connected to the breech block and as it moves it first of all unlocks the block and then pulls it clear of the breech and to the rear, compressing the return spring. The sequence of loading actions then takes place and all the parts return forwards again, the piston finally moving on a short extra distance under the force of the spring and, in its

last movement, locking the breech once again. Gas operation is popular for rifles and light machine guns because it is light and the amount of gas can be controlled easily, so varying the rate of fire or overcoming the drag of fouling or dirt. Barrel changing is less easy than with recoil because of the gas cylinder and piston, but it can be overcome without too much difficulty, and a good example of a successful barrel-changing gun is the British Bren.

The final method is blowback, which is almost self-explanatory. Blowback operation has progressed considerably

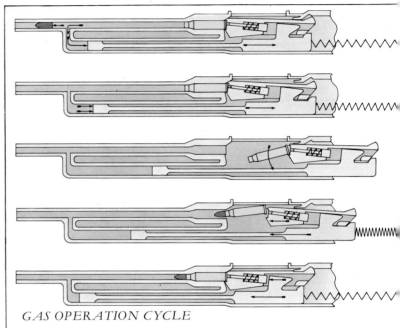

GAS OPERATION CYCLE

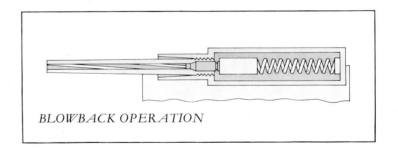

BLOWBACK OPERATION

since the end of World War II, so the following remarks are only related to the weapons described in this book – in the war years the system was much less powerful than today. In effect, blowback action uses no lock on the breech at all, but relies on the mass of the bolt to keep the breech safely closed until the bullet has left the muzzle. In fact it is not quite as simple as that in every case, but for some pistols using low-power rounds that description holds literally true: it works because the force of the burning powder lasts for so short a time that it is all over before the breech block overcomes its inertia and moves a significant distance. All practical submachine guns use blowback, but there are certain requirements for success. The first is that the cartridge must not be too powerful, hence submachine guns use similar rounds to pistols. The second is that the cartridge case must have parallel-sided walls – in other words the case is a true cylinder in shape. This is necessary so that it seals off the breech even when not entirely home in the chamber. With a tapered case like that in a rifle, the slightest movement backwards opens a gap all round the case and allows gas to escape, but with blowback the case is intended to move.

The diagram shows the essential features of the system. The case can be seen moving out of the breech, but still sealing it against any gas pressure. This would be the arrangement in a simple automatic pistol. With submachine guns there are usually some subtle changes. The simpler submachine guns have a fixed firing pin on the face of the bolt. The bolt is quite massive – half a kilogramme or so – and has feed guides and an extractor on it. All these guns fire from an open breech, that is, the bolt is held at the rear and released on pulling the trigger. As the bolt comes forward it picks up a round from the magazine and feeds it into the breech. As it closes up on the breech face the primer lines up with the fixed firing pin, and is struck just before the bolt reaches the face of the breech; in other words, the cartridge fires while the breech is still open. The bolt now continues forward while the powder pressure builds up, and this pressure slows down the bolt until, in a good design, the bolt face just touches the breech face and then starts backwards again. There is much fine judgement in this arrangement and the distances and times involved are very critical. The cartridge is fired when there is about three quarters of a millimetre still to travel. The powder pressure builds up in about one thousandth of a second, and at peak pressure there must not be too much case left sticking out of the breech, or it will burst. The success of the system depends on a balance between gun and ammunition design, and any changes in the ammunition will upset the working, so any one submachine gun is designed to use one type of ammunition. For the great majority of World War II models this was 9mm Parabellum, which was also a very general pistol round.

The system just described is called advanced primer ignition (API) and is only used in submachine guns. It has the advantage that it allows the bolt to be about half the weight of the simple blowback arrangement, since the cartridge expends half its power in overcoming the forward energy of the moving bolt. Using only simple blowback, the bolt to hold a 9mm Parabellum cartridge would need to weigh something like $1\frac{1}{2}$ kilogrammes, and its backward motion would take some stopping. Gun movement would be violent, to say the least, and the necessary strength in the body and springs would involve a good deal of extra weight.

The disadvantage of API blowback is the time taken for the bolt to move forward when firing the first shot. It has to fly forward the length of the body, and this often puts off the firer's aim, but there is no way of preventing this and it just has to be accepted. On automatic fire the movement of the gun is naturally considerable, and most tend to climb upwards. There have been any number of ideas to reduce this climb, most of them being a sort of directional port at the muzzle to deflect the gas blast and make it correct the climb.

They don't really work. The simple blowback pistol has no such problems as it always fires from a closed breech and uses some sort of hammer or firing pin for the ignition.

Before finally leaving the subject of mechanisms it might be as well to consider just what the designer is trying to do with his system. Automatic weapons such as machine guns are remarkably powerful and fast-moving pieces of machinery, and they cope with tremendous forces and loadings. An ordinary machine gun fires typical full-power rounds (i.e. about .30in or 7.62mm) at a rate of 600 per minute. In one minute the propellant powder produces 177 horsepower. Most of this is given out in heat and gas blast from the muzzle, but 44 horsepower are used to actually drive the bullets out of the barrel. Ten rounds are fired every second, which means that ten times in each second the mechanism goes through the actions of locking, firing, unlocking, extracting, ejecting, cocking, feeding and chambering. The bolt makes twenty movements, each one of a length slightly longer than that of a complete round. There is little actual time available for all this movement, since everything has to come to a halt for long enough to allow each round to fire. In fact, in this typical machine gun the bolt reaches a maximum speed of roughly 14mph (20km/h) on each to and fro run, and the return spring must be able to absorb this movement, slow it down and then reverse it forwards again to the same speed. The loadings on the individual parts can be enormous, yet each one must be small, light and reliable. Everything must be packed into the smallest possible space and capable of being carried by a man without fatigue, yet able to survive working in mud, dust or ice and snow.

Next there is the matter of heat. Each cartridge puts out a huge quantity of heat and a great deal of it goes into the metal of the breech and barrel. Unless there is some arrangement to take this heat away, the barrel will soon get red-hot and the inside of the bore will actually melt. In most of the early machine guns, particularly the Maxim family, the barrel was cooled by a water-jacket. This is both efficient and effective, but it involves complication and weight. However, water-cooled barrels can fire many thousands of rounds without ever getting dangerously hot, and they have been popular in medium machine guns which give supporting fire. The alternative method is air-cooling. This is lighter and easier, but it is nowhere near as effective except in unusual circumstances such as aircraft mountings where there is a steady air-blast.

In normal infantry guns the barrel gets hot very quickly, even when it has fins, and the only practical solutions are either to make the barrel massive and heavy so that it can absorb a good deal of heat, or to make it easy to change it, or both. The German MG 42 had a fairly heavy barrel capable of taking plenty of use, but it could also be changed very quickly and easily even when almost red-hot. Some other designs failed miserably to make any allowance for taking hold of the hot barrel when changing it, and seem to have relied on the recruiting sergeant's producing gunners with asbestos hands. But the heat is not entirely confined to the barrel alone. It travels along the metal of the body and breech block and warms up all the working parts, so that after a few hundred rounds the entire gun is substantially hotter than when it started. This heat affects the clearances between moving parts, and also can reduce the effectiveness of the many little springs which operate the various components. So the lot of the machine-gun designer is not necessarily a happy one.

Lastly, before we turn to the actual weapons themselves, a word about ammunition supply is necessary. Technically this is known as the feed system. There are two basic kinds, magazine and belt. Magazines are sheet metal boxes holding

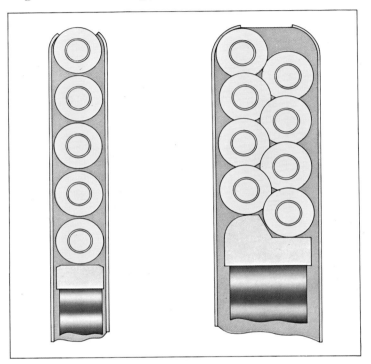

from five to fifty rounds in a vertical column, the column being a single row, or staggered, or in rare cases a double row. At the top of the box are two curved lips which allow the rounds to pass through one at a time. At the bottom is a false floor with a spring beneath it, pushing the rounds upwards against the lips. The bolt rides over the top round, but when it is fully back the top round pops up in front of it and is stripped out with the forward movement. There is a small ramp leading into the chamber, and the round slides up it and into the breech. Magazines are used in pistols, rifles, most submachine guns and a few light machine guns; they are light, robust, simple and easy to load. In an automatic weapon they suffer from the disadvantage that they severely limit the ammunition supply and need to be changed frequently, and with a fast-firing submachine gun this can be a nuisance.

Belt feed is self-evident from its name: the rounds are strung along a belt and joined either by a fabric strip or metal links. The fabric strip belt was pioneered by Maxim and is not entirely satisfactory since it is bulky and can absorb damp, which affects the ammunition, but its main

drawback is that the rounds are held in pockets sewn in the fabric and each round has to be withdrawn backwards out of its pocket before it can be chambered. This leads to complications inside the gun, and also gives rise to stoppages. However, if necessary, it can be reloaded by hand in the field, and the metal link belt cannot. Metal link belts allow the rounds to be pushed out forwards and the links fall away separately and are discarded. This sort of belt is easier to handle inside the gun, but both types require more mechanism than with a magazine since there has to be an arrangement of pawls and cams to pull the belt through for each successive round. A belt carries far more rounds than any magazine, but is both bulky and heavy to carry and it needs to be laid

Below: British troops pose in 1940 with Thompsons, most of them with the outdated drum magazine.

out in a box alongside the gun to allow easy feeding. This means that it is not well suited to a light machine gun that has to be carried by one man. The Germans managed to move their MG 34 and 42 without too much trouble, but they always had a two-man team to do it, and sometimes three.

As with all other features of small arms there have been some aberrations in the matter of ammunition feed. One is the special type of magazine known as the drum. This is an attempt to carry a useful number of rounds for a submachine

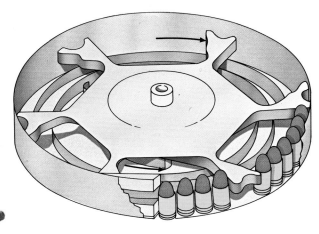

Above right: A water-cooled Browning M1917A1 in Italy, 1943. This is obviously a posed picture, as the gun has neither an ammunition belt nor a condenser can!

Right: The M1919A4 air-cooled version of the above gun. The tripod is much smaller and lighter, and the entire gun is now more mobile.

gun and it is mainly famous for its use on the US Thompson and the Soviet PPSh-41. In a drum magazine the rounds are held in a spiral and pushed out by a clock spring which has to be wound up by hand after loading. Drums are heavy and clumsy things to carry, and while they do give the firer a useful reserve of ammunition – 50 rounds in the Thompson and 72 in the PPSh-41 – they negate the advantages of light weight and easy handling that a submachine gun offers. They are also more prone to damage than simple box magazines. The US Army soon gave them up, although the Soviets held on to the end of the war.

Another feed system is the metal strip. This was pioneered by Hotchkiss before World War I and adopted by the Japanese in their Nambu design of machine gun. The strip is a flat framework of thin metal carrying a number of rounds (usually 30) held on to the top surface by pressed-out clips. Really it is a short piece of rigid metal belt, and it is fed in the same way. It appears to combine the disadvantages of the magazine and the belt, with the additional hazard that it is flimsy and easily damaged and does not protect the ammunition from dirt.

GERMANY

In World War I the infantry had been the predominant arm in all armies, none more so than in Germany, but at the beginning of World War II there was no doubt that the emphasis lay with the new armoured formations, and they got the best of whatever was going. However, despite this change of priority inside the army, it was the army which had the pick of all the small arms. The Luftwaffe and the navy, both of which had a need for personal weapons, particularly pistols, had to take a back seat and be content with a variety of weapons, usually non-standard, often ex-civilian, and frequently captured from the occupied countries. It did not seem to affect them much, but it did mean that there was a wide spread of demands for spare parts and ammunition.

The pre-war policy with regard to infantry weapons had not been very adventurous except for machine guns,

which were recognized to be the main firepower of the battalion. By using German-owned foreign firms such as Solothurn in Switzerland it was possible to continue development despite the Versailles Treaty restrictions. As a result, when the Wermacht was re-formed in 1934 there was the basis of a family of small arms on which to build. The German attitude was that a machine gun had to have a high rate of fire and be belt-fed. Although they took some of the magazine-fed ZB series into service when stocks ran short in 1942 and 1943, they never made one themselves. Instead, the MG 34 and 42 were made to fill two roles, that of the light gun in the section and as a support gun at company level also. By giving the guns quick-change barrels they could keep up a rapid rate of fire for quite long periods, and so they became what is now known in NATO as the General Purpose Machine Gun, and they were remarkably effective too. Extremely high rates of fire never caught on with the Allies, who considered them a waste of ammunition, yet they were keen enough to use the guns when they captured them. The wisdom of this emphasis on the machine gun was demonstrated time and time again in Russia, where the only answer to the massed swarms of Soviet infantry was a fast-

firing gun and plenty of ammunition.

Having stuck to designs laid down before the war, the Germans were never averse to trying out new ideas once the actual fighting had started. One of the puzzling features of the German war effort is the amount of time, money and labour that was diverted to bright ideas while the country was in the middle of the most dreadful crises. A good example is self-loading rifles, though there are plenty of others in such areas as aircraft and missiles.

Having made the decision to stay with the bolt-action Mauser, the German Army let two contracts for self-loading rifles in 1940. At the same time the Luftwaffe were putting out contracts for their FG 42 and competing for the same factory space. Next came the two 1942 self-loaders, the Haenel and Walther designs, of which the Haenel was adopted, and finally the series of Gewehr 43s, culminating in the excellent Sturmgewehr of 1944. But this was not a reasoned, steady development process, as one might suppose, for at each stage quite substantial numbers of weapons were made and issued into service, and a good deal of effort was wasted on the unsuccessful models. True to the German concept, each design went to competitive tender, but the loser could be sure of getting an order of some sort to compensate him for the money and effort he had spent in

Below: A soldier armed with an MG 34 machine gun and MP 38 submachine gun on the outskirts of Stalingrad.

developing his weapon. So it was a competitive tender in which nobody lost! This sort of luxury has no place in an all-out war, but Germany took some time to realize that it was an all-out war, and actually cancelled a number of war contracts after the fall of France because it was thought that the war was over.

Despite an air of overwhelming national organization and Nazi efficiency within the country, Germany was not well organized at all in manufacturing terms until late in World War II. Up to the middle of 1943 the country's industry was working at about 60% effectiveness for the war effort, and it was not until Albert Speer really got hold of the reins of industrial power and was able to direct labour where he needed it and direct the factories to make armaments to a national plan that any sort of coherent and sensible production output began to appear. From then on until the end of the war the production from the German factories was amazing, and was far less bothered by bombing than the Allies believed. In fact, in some factories, production improved by leaps and bounds. Mauser turned out more machine guns in 1944 than in any other year of the war.

Probably the biggest contribution made by the German designers in World War II was in using modern methods of manufacture. Before 1940 small arms were made by the time-hallowed process of machining out solid metal. It was Germany which took the lead in using the techniques of the motor trade to build weapons – an idea that soon caught on.

When the home industries could not keep pace, factories in the occupied countries were brought in to fill the gaps. Some of them made German weapons, others made their own designs and these were taken into German service. It was not a policy that would have endeared itself to ordnance supply officers, particularly when it came to getting spare parts and replacements, but it meant that there were always enough weapons to go round.

The German infantry battalions who used all this equipment were always smaller than those of the Allies, and in 1944, when the toll of the war was clearly apparent, all formations were reduced in size to conform with the smaller numbers of troops available. So the battalion came down to 653 men, when Allied battalions were carrying one or two hundred more. These 653 were armed with the following small arms; 436 rifles, 111 pistols, 105 submachine guns, and 33 machine guns. The total of these weapons comes to 685, the difference being explained by the fact that the machine gunners carried a pistol as well. The large number of pistols is interesting, since there were only 16 officers on the establishment, and when these are added to the machine gunners, they leave 62 pistols being carried by NCOs and weapon crews. This battalion was organized into three rifle companies with three platoons in each, and 10 machine guns altogether in the company. A weapons company contained the 81mm mortars and 8 heavy machine guns. It was a streamlined and rather thin organization, lacking in proper backing and mobility, but well suited to a defensive war – and that was all that it was ever called upon to fight.

Pistols

German military pistols are probably better known and more has been written about them than any others. There is a sort of cult about German pistols, in which the Luger holds particular pride of place. It is a little difficult to understand the attraction since the pistols themselves are no better and no worse than many others, but it may stem from the fact that they are distinctive in shape and unlike most others that have been used. The German Army adopted automatic pistols early on in the twentieth century and stayed with the same patterns throughout the two world wars, so that enormous numbers of them were made and captured by the Allied side. In this study we shall only be able to examine the three most popular and widespread models, namely the Parabellum 08 (Luger), the Mauser and the Walther P 38, but there were many others in service. More German servicemen carried pistols than did the Allies, since a holster was almost part of the uniform.

Although the standard pistol ammunition was 9mm Parabellum, there were never enough 9mm pistols to equip all the services, and 7.65mm was a common alternative. The SS and police used 7.65mm pistols of several different makes

– so did the Luftwaffe – and there was a fair supply of these weapons since the German police had always been armed, and there was an existing industry geared to making weapons in that size. German officers were not discouraged from buying their own pistols, and many of them, particularly the staff officers, chose the smaller 7.65mm sizes.

In the infantry, pistols were carried by men whose task prevented them from using a rifle. These were the signallers, machine gunners and mortar crews. Paratroopers all carried one because their other weapons were dropped in containers

Mauser C96		
Ammunition	7.63mm Mauser Patrone	
Length	12.25in	312mm
Weight unloaded	2lb 12oz	1.25kg
Barrel	5.5in	139mm
Magazine	10-round integral box	
Muzzle velocity	1425ft/sec	434m/sec

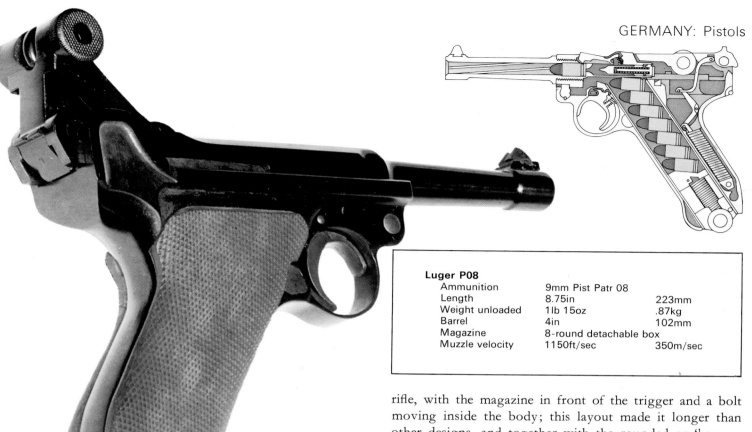

Luger P08

Ammunition	9mm Pist Patr 08	
Length	8.75in	223mm
Weight unloaded	1lb 15oz	.87kg
Barrel	4in	102mm
Magazine	8-round detachable box	
Muzzle velocity	1150ft/sec	350m/sec

and might take some time to find on the drop zone. Naval boarding and landing parties carried them, and so did many of the officers and senior petty officers when on shore. All Luftwaffe aircrew were armed, for their own protection if shot down, and all crews of armoured vehicles carried pistols also.

The numbers of pistols in service was enormous and the load on German industry to make them was equally large. Under these circumstances it is not surprising that it was impossible to keep to one type. There was a miscellany of models and types spread among the three services, with three main ones predominating – the Mauser, Luger, and Walther.

The Mauser C 96 was one of the oldest pistols used in World War II and was issued on a limited scale to the German Army. It had never been officially adopted, although 150,000 were made by Mauser in World War I in 9mm calibre when it was realized that Germany was desperately short of small arms. These pistols were still in store, or at least many of them were, in 1939, and were re-issued to units. The Mauser was a large and powerful pistol, originally built for a high-velocity 7.63mm special cartridge, and the mechanism was easily able to cope with the stresses of 9mm Parabellum when it was re-barrelled. It was in some ways like a miniature

rifle, with the magazine in front of the trigger and a bolt moving inside the body; this layout made it longer than other designs, and together with the rounded or 'broom-handle' butt it had an ugly and clumsy appearance. In fact, it was anything but clumsy, and it shot well and accurately. The operating system was recoil, using a short locking block to connect the barrel and bolt. The return spring was quite strong, and it pushed both bolt and barrel forward in its last movement, completing the locking action at the same time.

The Mauser was unusual in that it normally had a large hollow wooden holster which doubled as a carbine butt when it was clipped to the bottom of the stock. While undoubtedly useful, this made for a remarkably clumsy burden when slung on a belt and it can scarcely be described as entirely practical. The sights were quite elaborate and the sliding backsight could be adjusted up to 1,000m, at which range the bullet was likely to be neither accurate nor dangerous, but at lesser ranges the pistol shot surprisingly well in the carbine form. A small number were made as machine pistols with the ability to shoot automatically, and for these the magazine was enlarged to 20 rounds from the usual 10. As with all such conversions, the performance was poor and scarcely worth the effort.

The drawback to the Mauser was the cost of manufacture; designed in the days when weapons were built by craftsmen, the amount of machining and skilled fitting required in its construction made it unsuitable for mass production and none were actually made during World War II.

The second pistol in general issue was the Parabellum 08, or Luger as it was called after its designer, and there is no space here to go into the many different versions which were produced to special order throughout its long life, and in some cases are still being made. There have been many excellent books about this pistol, and there has also been more rubbish spoken and printed about it than any other military weapon. It was a strange design, old in concept and an anomaly in operation. It was designed at the time when the Maxim machine gun was being considered by practically every army in the world, and one is tempted to think that Borchardt, whose mechanism the Luger used, was influenced by the success of the Maxim. Anyway, he took much the same toggle-joint mechanism for his breech locking and used recoil to unlock it, the toggles breaking upwards. This arrangement is good when it is balanced to the ammunition, and with 9mm Parabellum the action works well, but with other varieties it can jam easily and sometimes damage itself. The remainder of the mechanism, particularly the trigger system, was over-complicated and delicate.

However, the Luger was a delight to handle and balanced as few others have ever done. It was generally issued to the German Army from 1908 onwards, but by 1936 it was realized that its days were ending, and a simpler and cheaper type was needed. Despite this, production continued in the Mauser plant at Oberndorf until June 1942, and it remained in service until 1945. It was enormously popular with its German users, some of whom are reported as being unwilling to give it up for the P 38, but that may be no more than a modern legend.

The official pistol of the German forces throughout World War II was the Walther P 38, a workmanlike, robust and straightforward 9mm automatic based on a reliable recoil system of operation and reasonably easy to make. It has the useful feature that it is double-action, meaning that it can be carried with a round in the breech and the hammer forward, resting against a safety stop. It is thus completely safe. When the trigger is pulled the hammer first cocks then fires, after which the pistol acts in the normal way. This double-action overcame the last objection to automatic pistols, namely that they needed two hands to fire the first shot (i.e. one to pull the slide back). The magazine holds eight rounds, the same as the Luger, and the feel and accuracy are very nearly as good.

In fact the P 38 was an immensely successful design, and it is still in service with the German Army. It was carried by the great majority of front-line troops in World War II, and was a popular trophy among Allied soldiers. Reliability is good, maintenance easy, and jams few since it is tolerant of variations in its ammunition.

Above: A German soldier rounds up prisoners with his Parabellum 08 (Luger) pistol.

Walther P38		
Ammunition	9mm Pist Patr 08	
Length	8.38 in	213mm
Weight unloaded	2 lb 2 oz	.96kg
Barrel	5 in	127mm
Magazine	8-round detachable box	
Muzzle velocity	1,150 ft/sec	350m/sec

Hand-Operated Rifles

Any description of hand-operated rifles in Germany in World War II is largely confined to Mausers, since that make formed by far the majority of those that were used. They were by 1939 a venerable design, having originated in the 1890s, and had been in service ever since adoption in 1904. These Mauser rifles had set the standard of accuracy and good workmanship up to World War I, and the pattern had been copied or built under licence throughout the world.

The standard German Army rifle in 1939 was the Mauser model of 1898 and a shortened version first brought out in 1935. Neither was in any way revolutionary by that time – indeed they were remarkably conservative in their design, and it seems unfortunate that the German General Staff did not take their chance in 1935 and modernize what was by then a weapon with known failings. They were probably restrained by two powerful factors; first, that in 1935 German industry was already feeling the pinch of re-armament and there were the first signs of lack of factory space; second, the fact that the design had been so phenomenally successful in selling round the world that it no doubt seemed silly to change for the sake of change.

The Mauser Model 98 was a long-barrelled rifle in the best traditions of the late nineteenth century. Its main claim to fame lay in its neat system of forward-locking lugs which allowed the body to be relatively light since it took no firing

Above: Taking aim with the Mauser 98K carbine, the most common infantry weapon of the German forces.

stresses, and also made for greater accuracy and consistency in shooting. The drawback to the forward-locking arrangement is that it requires a longer bolt travel than the rear system such as the Enfields enjoyed, and the Mausers were always renowned for having a slow bolt-action.

The 1935 model was no more than the 1898 one cut down, shortened and lightened. It only changed in dimensions, and retained the same slow bolt-action and also the same five-round magazine. The magazine was a strange feature, since it must have been obvious to the German General Staff that it was too small. It would have not needed much alteration of the design to put in ten rounds, but this was not done, and it counted against the battle-worthiness of the weapon thereafter. The general outline of the Model 98 Karabiner, or 98K as it is generally known, was quite attractive. It was a slim, well-proportioned short rifle with the stock cut back from the muzzle, and the semi-pistol grip stock of its predecessor, but unfortunately it was a relatively awkward rifle to shoot, and the bolt action was most disappointing. The sight radius was short, which did not make for good shooting, and the effective range was less than that quoted for most other rifles in the same class.

Far right: SS troops on parade with the long-barrelled Gewehr 98 rifle, less popular with the soldiers than the more widely issued carbine version.

The really surprising thing about the 98K is that it ever appeared at all. It should never have been made as late as 1935; there were already plenty of good self-loading rifles in the world at that time, and it was well within the capabilities of the German manufacturers to have made one at least as good as the Garand. Had they done so, the fire effect of the German infantry section would have been very different from what it was.

Infanteriegewehr Modell 1898 (Mauser 98)

Ammunition	7.92mm Gewehr Patrone 1898	
Length	49.9in	1255mm
Weight unloaded	9lb	4.14kg
Barrel	29.15in	740mm
Magazine	5-round internal box	
Muzzle velocity	2850ft/sec	870m/sec

The 98K was the basic weapon of all soldiers who were not specialists. It can be seen in practically every photograph of German soldiers taken during the war, and it served throughout without changing in any but the slightest features. Sniping versions were made by carefully selecting a good weapon and fitting a telescope, though the 98K was never a target rifle and the fitting of a telescope did nothing to improve the accuracy of the basic weapon. Later on in the war, as materials became scarcer, the quality began to decline, and the models built in 1943 and after show decided lacks in finish and fitting. Mass production ended in 1944 when the remaining small-arms industry turned to cheaper and more easily made weapons. But despite a full production line in the Mauser factory and at least three others in the occupied countries there were never enough to go round, and the

Karabiner Modell 1898k (Kar 98K)

Ammunition	7.92mm Gewehr Patrone 1898	
Length	43.6in	1110mm
Weight unloaded	8lb 9oz	3.9 kg
Barrel	23.6in	600mm
Magazine	5-round integral box	
Muzzle velocity	2450ft/sec	745m/sec

independent services such as the Luftwaffe were forced to use other types.

In the case of the Luftwaffe they armed their ground troops with a Hungarian rifle built for them in Budapest. It was the 1935 Hungarian model of an elderly Mannlicher and it was perfectly serviceable, if not modern. It was re-barrelled to the German 7.92mm calibre and produced from 1940 for the remainder of the war. In Czechoslovakia the current Czech version of the Mauser was modified and shortened and that too was pressed into service. This particular weapon was shortened rather too far for use by mountain troops and it gave a harsh kick and a large muzzle flash when fired.

Finally there was the Austrian version, which again went to the Luftwaffe. This rifle was perhaps the best of all the Mausers of World War II since it was a military version of a commercial sporting rifle, and it had fewer of the vices of the German mass-produced ones. The finish was far better and the bolt action smoother, but the constricting five-round magazine remained unchanged.

Summarizing the German hand-operated rifles of the war, one has to say that they were uninspired and indifferent in performance. The German infantryman got less than he deserved. Whereas Allied soldiers were often only too willing to use captured machine guns, there are practically no examples of any employing Mausers against their previous owners.

Self-Loading Rifles

As we have seen in the section dealing with hand-operated rifles, Germany decided to re-arm in 1935 with a design that was virtually 40 years old and accept the limitations that this would impose on her infantry. The decision was surprising in view of the technical achievements and industrial ability of the country, but most of these resources were required for the more complicated weapons and vehicles, and the Mauser was well known. Yet Germany had used a self-loading rifle in 1914; this was the Mondragon, made in Switzerland to a Mexican design, which was bought by Germany and used mainly as an observer's gun in early warplanes. Despite the official view that bolt-action rifles were good enough, some research had been done during the post-war years and some small contracts had been let out for development work. In particular, a lower-powered cartridge was investigated; it had been realized since 1917 that the standard 7.92mm rounds were far more powerful than was normally needed in war. However, things moved slowly until 1938, when the threat of war put a spurt into most of the armaments industry, but it was a bit late by then and in 1940 a further special programme was needed with the intention of producing a self-loading rifle in two years.

The first models appeared in 1941, made by the firms of Walther and Mauser. They were almost identical except for the mechanism and method of locking, and neither was entirely satisfactory. They were heavy and expensive to make,

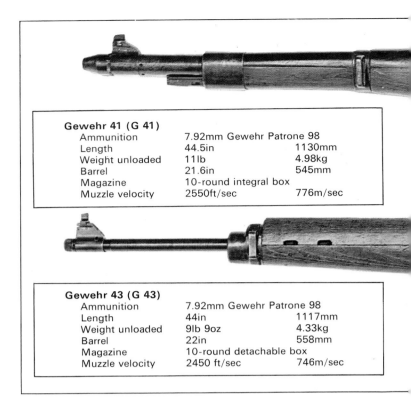

Gewehr 41 (G 41)

Ammunition	7.92mm Gewehr Patrone 98	
Length	44.5in	1130mm
Weight unloaded	11lb	4.98kg
Barrel	21.6in	545mm
Magazine	10-round integral box	
Muzzle velocity	2550ft/sec	776m/sec

Gewehr 43 (G 43)

Ammunition	7.92mm Gewehr Patrone 98	
Length	44in	1117mm
Weight unloaded	9lb 9oz	4.33kg
Barrel	22in	558mm
Magazine	10-round detachable box	
Muzzle velocity	2450 ft/sec	746m/sec

but the Walther design was adopted and put into service as the Gewehr 41 (W), or G 41. It saw service in small numbers on the Russian and Italian fronts, but it was only a partial success; it was poorly balanced and too heavy, the magazine was fixed, which was awkward, and the gas system was difficult to clean. An improved model appeared in 1943, called, not surprisingly, the G 43. In this the gas system was greatly simplified and lightened, the magazine was made detachable, and a mounting for telescopic sights was built into the body. All of these changes were straight copies from the Soviet Tokarev Model 40, which had impressed the Germans in the Russian campaign.

The G 43 was a much better proposition than the G 41 and when it went into production in 1943 every effort was made to simplify manufacture. It was issued as a sniper rifle, and was never intended to replace the Mauser 98K. It was used on all the battle fronts, but only as a specialist weapon, and the numbers made were quite small. It offered nothing in its design, and was no advance on conventional practice. In fact, it much resembled the US Garand.

A far more significant advance was the parachutist's rifle, the Fallschirmjaeger Gewehr Model 1942 or FG 42. This remarkable rifle was specially produced for the Luftwaffe's paratroops to give them the extra firepower that they needed when operating in small detached groups. It was actually the first of what are now called assault rifles, and it was very nearly a complete success, despite the handicap of firing the old type 7.92mm full-power round. The design was among the outstanding ones of the war, and it deserved a better fate than it got. It was a selective-fire rifle, capable of full automatic or single-shot fire. It had a bipod to steady it and a 20-shot magazine feeding from the left side. The mechanism

was so good that it was copied and used as the basis for the present US M 60 machine gun, but as a rifle the FG 42 just failed. A series of circumstances prevented it ever being fully developed, and probably no more than 7,000 were ever produced. However, it was issued to parachutists and its first use was in the dramatic rescue of Mussolini by glider. Like the G 43, the FG 42 was never made in sufficient numbers to replace any other service weapons, and it never made any impact on the conduct or outcome of the war. It was a pleasant rifle to fire, though at automatic it was too light and tended to walk away from the firer, moving to the right despite the bipod. The straight-line layout made it easy to control when fired as a hand-held rifle and the sights were particularly good. The FG 42 was lighter than a G 41 and a far better weapon in every way, but most expensive and time-consuming to make, and by 1943 Germany could not

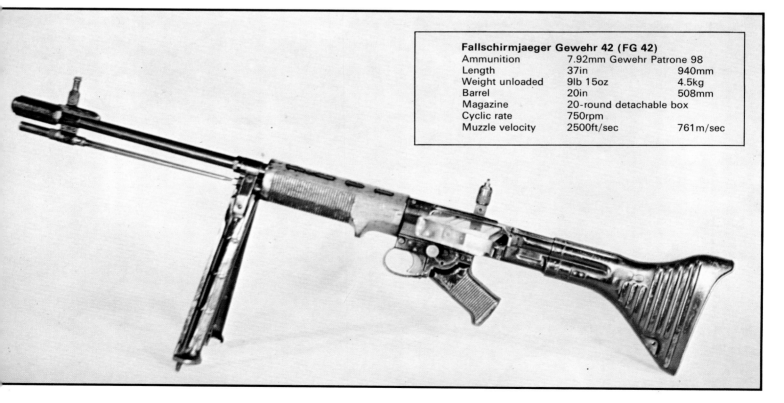

Fallschirmjaeger Gewehr 42 (FG 42)		
Ammunition	7.92mm Gewehr Patrone 98	
Length	37in	940mm
Weight unloaded	9lb 15oz	4.5kg
Barrel	20in	508mm
Magazine	20-round detachable box	
Cyclic rate	750rpm	
Muzzle velocity	2500ft/sec	761m/sec

afford to spend much time in rifle manufacture. Quantity was the order of the day, and the FG 42, for all its excellence, lost out.

The next series of self-loading rifles used the lower-powered round which we mentioned at the beginning of this section. This round was another quick design job; it was virtually a cut-down 7.92mm cartridge case with a shorter bullet. The result was a lower-velocity bullet, but one which still had plenty of power in it. This sort of compromise is usually a recipe for disaster but this time it worked, and the round was adopted as the 'Kurz' or short round, officially the 7.92mm Pistole Patrone 43. It was a great success and several rifles were specially designed to use it, the work starting in 1940, almost before the round was ready. In the usual German system two firms were given the same contract, and both made small quantities. This weapon became the MK 42 (Maschinen Karabiner Model 1942), and was issued to troops on the Russian front during the winter of 1942/43. The Haenel design was found to be better operationally and easier to make, so it was further developed and put into volume production as the MK 43 and so stayed until 1944, by which time over 300,000 had been made. The MK 43 was intended to become the basic infantry weapon of the entire German Army, replacing the bolt-action rifles and submachine guns, and the first issues were to élite units such as the SS.

Allied troops first met the MK 43 in the Ardennes offensive of December 1944 and it is significant that it was then used by the 1st and 12th SS Panzer Divisions and the Fuehrer Escort Brigade, while the line infantry still carried 98Ks and a few G 43s. Later models of the MK 43 were renamed Sturmgewehr 44 (Assault Rifle Model 1944), though the design barely changed. It was an all-metal weapon with minimal furniture and all parts intended for decentralized manufacture by small firms. It was not particularly pretty to look at, nor was it attractive to hold. However, it shot very well and recoil was tolerable and controllable. On automatic

fire the muzzle climbed slightly, but not excessively, and the burst could be kept fairly near the target, there being, of course, no bipod. It was popular with the German soldiers, none of whom saw much attraction in the 98K, and the only criticism that can be levelled at the MK 43 is that it was slightly heavy. The MK 43 was fitted with a variety of accessories, and this was the rifle which was given the remarkable adaptor which allowed for shooting round corners, the 'Krummer Lauf' or curved barrel. One which gave a 30° angle was meant for street and trench fighting, and a 90° one was carried on a few tanks for clearing off troublesome infantry on the decks and roof. With a special prism sight these curious devices were quite successful, provided one did not want to fire too many rounds, since the barrel soon wore out. Another experiment was the use of infra-red night sights; about 300 MKs were fitted with these and used at the very end of the war for night sniping at short range, a development which was followed up with considerable interest after the war on both sides of the Iron Curtain.

Above: *An MK 43 fitted with the 'Krummer Lauf' for firing around corners or out of trenches.*

Maschinen Karabiner 43 (MK 43)

Ammunition	7.92mm Pist Patr 43	
Length	37in	940mm
Weight unloaded	11lb 4oz	5.1kg
Barrel	16.5in	418mm
Magazine	30-round detachable box	
Cyclic rate	500rpm	
Muzzle velocity	2125ft/sec	647m/sec

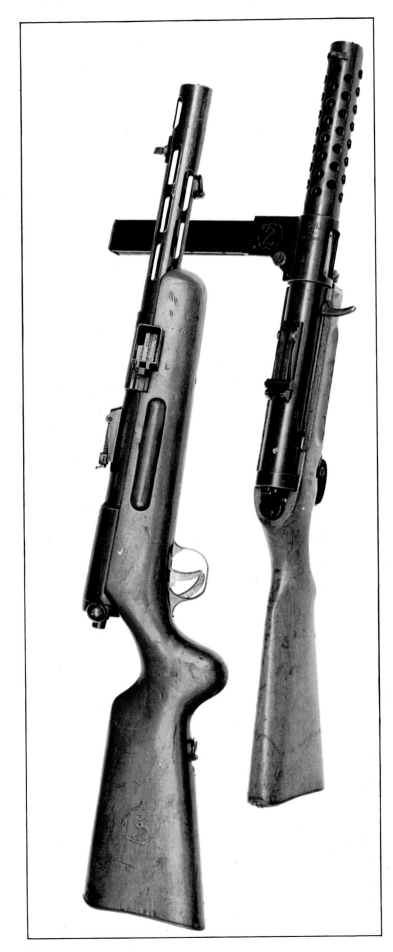

Submachine Guns

Although Italy first used submachine guns in action the German Army was not far behind, and it is a matter for academic discussion as to which country first used them in their proper role as one-man close-quarter weapons. Certainly that was in the minds of the German High Command, who laid down the specification in 1916, and it was in the mind of Hugo Schmeisser, who designed and made the first one. This venerable weapon was first put into service in March 1918 and as a result was christened the Maschinen Pistole 1918, or MP 18. It was carried in small numbers in the successful German spring offensive of that year, though for some reason the obvious lessons were not immediately learnt by either side.

In post-war Germany submachine guns were banned except for police, who carried the MP 18 in modified form and who were responsible for its being redesigned and improved in 1928, when it became the MP 28. The magazine was completely changed to give a 32-round box, carrying the rounds in a staggered row, and this fact is significant, because this type of box became more or less standard on German submachine guns, and it gave rise to a lot of trouble later. But the MP 28 could not be made in Germany, and manufacture was leased to Belgium and Switzerland, which turned them out in plenty and sold them all over the world. At the same time they sold them in Europe, and so enabled the German Army to conveniently capture them after 1940, thereby making up stocks at no cost.

Maschinen Pistole 34/I (Bergmann MP 34)		
Ammunition	9mm Pist Patr 08 (9mm Parabellum)	
Length	33in	840mm
Weight unloaded	8lb 15oz	4.5kg
Barrel	7.75in	196mm
Magazine	24- or 32-round detachable box	
Cyclic rate	650rpm	
Muzzle velocity	1250ft/sec	381m/sec

Both MP 18 and MP 28 were issued to the German Army in World War II, and it is extremely difficult to tell which was which. Most of the MP 18 guns were given a new magazine housing and so converted to the MP 28 magazine, and apart from trifling alterations in dimensions the two cannot be told apart. They are both straightforward guns, built in the traditional way, machined out of large pieces of solid steel with a one-piece wooden stock, long-range sights, and all the appearance of miniature rifles. They were simple, reliable and tremendously robust, but they suffered from being

Maschinen Pistole 28/II (MP28/II)		
Ammunition	9mm Parabellum	
Length	32in	812mm
Weight unloaded	8lb 12oz	3.97kg
Barrel	7.75in	196mm
Magazine	20-, 32-, or 50-round detachable box	
Cyclic rate	500rpm	
Muzzle velocity	1250ft/sec	381m/sec

heavy. Each one weighed roughly 9lb (4kg) unloaded, and this was as much as a bolt-action rifle. They were issued first of all to specialist and assault troops, and in fact only a few of the MP 18s or 28s got into the hands of the infantry divisions until later in the war when the production of the MP 40 became sufficiently large to replace the older veterans.

Another submachine gun of the old pattern was the Bergmann, which escaped the restrictions of the Versailles Treaty by being made outside the frontiers of Germany, in this case in Denmark. It was much like the Schmeissers at first glance, but in fact was more complicated mainly because it had a separate bolt to cock the action and this bolt stuck out from the back of the body in much the same way as on a rifle. The action of cocking was the same as a rifle also; one turned the bolt, pulled it back, pushed it forward and turned it down again. This complication was put in in order to try and keep the working parts clean, and it probably did, but at an uneconomical cost and weight. Another oddity was that the magazine stuck out to the right, and so when the gun was being fired the magazine was well clear of the firer's body to the right side, thus effectively making the man twice as wide as he need be, and so more difficult to conceal.

Apart from these features the Bergmann was quite straightforward and perfectly reliable. It was introduced as the MP 34, and quickly improved to the MP 35. The entire factory output was taken by the Waffen SS, who issued it as widely as possible throughout all ranks. It would seem that some of the issue models were converted to a left-hand magazine feed, though there are no records of this being done at the factory, so it may have been a local workshop modification.

In 1938 came the apotheosis of the German submachine-gun design, the Erma MP 38. This was probably the most famous submachine gun of the war and to the Allies it was known by the name of Schmeisser, which has since become almost a generic term for the species. In fact the MP 38 had nothing to owe to Hugo Schmeisser and was entirely an Erma design. It was the first to have a folding stock, the first to be made entirely without any wood anywhere on it – all the furniture was of steel or plastic – and the first to be specifically intended for use in vehicles. The magazine formed the forward hand-grip and the whole outline was of squat, single-minded purposefulness. It rapidly became the symbol of the German paratroopers and indeed it was one of their main weapons, but it was also issued widely throughout the army; and the demand soon outstripped the supply. In 1940 it was redesigned by Schmeisser to make it easier and cheaper to produce and he made an excellent job of it. The MP 40, as it was now called, was a little cruder than the MP 38, a little less refined, but just as robust and tough. It could be made in separate components and sub-assemblies which only needed to be brought together at the factory which finally assembled them, and as a result the output of this submachine gun was virtually immune to Allied bombing for the entire war. Thousands survived the war, many being taken into French service, and there are still some in the hands of guerillas and terrorists today.

The great advantage of the submachine gun to the German parachutist was that he could carry it with him when he

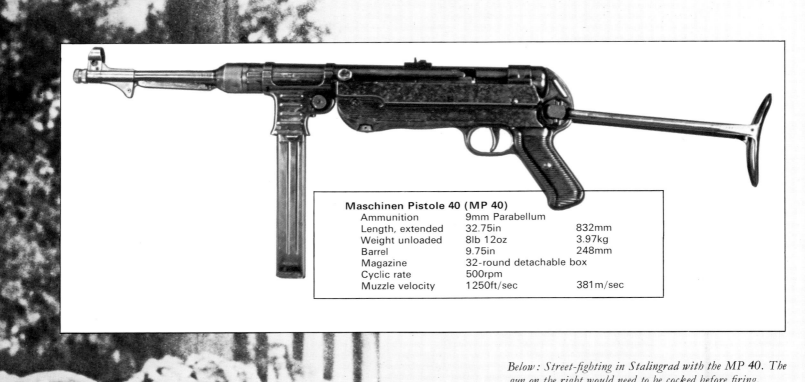

Maschinen Pistole 40 (MP 40)

Ammunition	9mm Parabellum	
Length, extended	32.75in	832mm
Weight unloaded	8lb 12oz	3.97kg
Barrel	9.75in	248mm
Magazine	32-round detachable box	
Cyclic rate	500rpm	
Muzzle velocity	1250ft/sec	381m/sec

Below: Street-fighting in Stalingrad with the MP 40. The gun on the right would need to be cocked before firing.

jumped. The German parachutes opened with a severe shock and the harness was fairly crude by Allied standards. The result was that any attempt to carry equipment or weapons usually ended with the load breaking away when the parachute opened, or hurting the man carrying it. The MP 38 and 40 were small and light enough to tuck under the harness without these drawbacks; they thus gave the man the benefit of immediate firepower as soon as he hit the ground. (Incidentally, stories of parachutists firing their submachine guns while in the air are quite untrue; no German jumped from sufficient height to allow time for that sort of thing.) So these submachine guns featured prominently in all the airborne operations of the war, though after Crete the troopers asked for something with a greater range since they had been severely handled on some of the drop zones by dug-in Bren guns and had been unable to reach back effectively. But this was one of the very few complaints ever raised against submachine guns.

In Russia there was some concern over the large drum magazine on the PPSh-41 and it was thought necessary to carry the same sort of ammunition supply on the MP 40 so that in a fire-fight the German soldier would not have to stop and reload more often than the enemy. The MP 40 could not possibly take a drum, so the quick wartime answer was to join two magazines together and modify the feed opening so that when one was empty the other could be slid sideways into line. The only check to firing was to pause, pull the bolt back, slide the magazine across, and carry on firing. Unfortunately it was not a success: it was too heavy, too clumsy and too prone to jams. Also, the second magazine was open to the elements, and in Russia this was fatal. Another trouble, and this applied to all MP 38 and 40 magazines, was that they used a single-column feed. Single column allowed more friction for each round as it fed down the magazine, and both submachine guns suffered from feed stoppages throughout their lives. Admittedly the remedial action was both quick and simple – merely turning the gun on its side and shaking it was usually enough – but it could be irritating and possibly fatal when in action.

Unlike other weapons, there were few captured submachine guns which could be taken into German service, although some Italian Berettas were bought in, so in general the submachine guns used in the Wermacht were German-made, and were sound, practical, workmanlike designs.

Machine Guns

Maxim 08		
Ammunition	7.92mm Gewehr 98	
Length	46.25in	1175mm
Weight unloaded	58lb 5oz	26.44kg
Barrel	28.3in	719mm
Magazine	250-round fabric belt	
Cyclic rate	300rpm	
Muzzle velocity	2925ft/sec	892m/sec

From the very beginning of machine guns, the German Army saw their possibilities as an infantry arm. In World War I it was usually the German machine guns which dominated no man's land, and in World War II they were equally prominent. The whole layout of the infantry section or squad was based on the machine gun, and the riflemen were seen not as a complementary group (which was how the British looked upon them) but as a supporting group for the gun. They kept the gun in action, for the gun was the firepower.

It was a sensible approach, and a realistic one, and it should have been copied by the Allies far earlier than it actually was. Nevertheless, the German evolvement of the tactical use of their guns was not easy, for they were forbidden to build any under the terms of the Versailles Treaty. As with so many other weapons this restriction was hardly effective, and active research into lighter and better guns continued throughout the 1920s in neighbouring countries such as Switzerland and Austria using German capital to finance local arms firms. Some tactical exercises were tried in Russia, though this was not always easy nor successful.

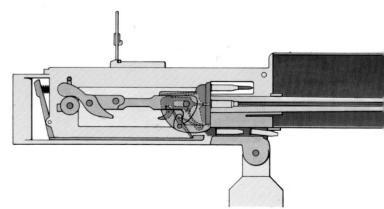

The World War I machine gun had been the Maxim, very similar to the British Vickers, water-cooled, heavy, and complicated and expensive to build. It was scarcely mobile without some sort of vehicle, and was quite useless to an infantry section having to move on its feet. The old Maxim at least possessed one great advantage – it was reliable.

Provided that it could be kept supplied with belts of ammunition and a little water for the barrel jacket, it could fire all day. It needed a team of at least three men to look after it, and in action there were generally at least four, so that it was expensive in manpower. The first-line units could not spare men on this scale nor could they tolerate the immobility, so the Maxim was given to reserve and fortification units where there was no need to move it and it could be left in a fixed mounting. Under these conditions a Maxim could be served by two men quite easily, and that was how many of them spent their war.

No German light machine gun came out of the First World War, and when the army expanded and re-equipped in the early 1930s the only practical mobile infantry machine gun was the 1917 Dreyse, which had been a water-cooled model. It was severely lightened and put into use until a promising Swiss design appeared from the firm of Solothurn. Perhaps it was no accident that Solothurn was financed by Rheinmetall, and there is some evidence to show that the

chosen gun was built to a specification that originated in Germany. However, it was taken by the Mauser factory and altered in some respects to better satisfy the needs of the new army. In particular, the magazine feed was abandoned and an improved belt feed inserted.

As soon as the Mauser production line began turning out the new gun it was taken into service as the Maschinengewehr Model 34, or MG 34, and it deserves a close inspection, for it represented a major change in the philosophy which up till then had surrounded machine guns. The MG 34 was far lighter than the old water-cooled models, and only a bit heavier than the light machine guns such as the Lewis and Hotchkiss, but the difference lay in its use, for it was meant to be a gun for all purposes and to double as a light and a medium machine gun. In 1934 this was a radical idea – indeed it was still so in 1939 – but it was proved to be correct throughout five years of war, and it is now accepted by NATO as being the way to use machine guns.

The MG 34 pushed the remaining Dreyses into storage and quickly became the standard machine gun of the German Army. It was an air-cooled weapon, belt-fed and capable of being fired from either a bipod (the usual way) or a tripod when sustained fire was needed. As a light gun the belt was

Maschinengewehr 34 (MG 34)

Ammunition	7.92mm Gewehr 98	
Length	48in	1219mm
Weight unloaded	26lb 11oz	12.1kg
Barrel	24.75in	627mm
Magazine	50-round belt or 75-round saddle drum	
Cyclic rate	800–900rpm	
Muzzle velocity	2480ft/sec	755m/sec

Below: An MG 34 in position on the Atlantic Wall.

Below: A machine-gun crew of the Leibstandarte Division in action with an MG 34 during the Balkan offensive of 1941.

Maschinengewehr 42 (MG 42)		
Ammunition	7.92mm Gewehr Patr 98	
Length	48in	1219mm
Weight unloaded	25lb 8oz	11.5kg
Barrel	21in	535mm
Magazine	50-round belt	
Cyclic rate	1200rpm	
Muzzle velocity	2480ft/sec	755m/sec

contained in a saddle-drum which held a 75-round belt and wound the empty portion onto a roller so that it did not hang down and interfere with movement. For a light gun this was another novelty, because until that time all light guns had been fed from magazines of one kind or another and had been restricted to about 30 rounds for each loading.

As a sustained-fire gun the MG 34 fired the usual type of long metal-linked belt and in this role was always mounted on its heavy tripod. Sustained firing heated the barrel, and this then had to be changed. Changing the barrel was one of the weak spots of the design as some care was needed to avoid getting burnt hands. The method was a little awkward as it was necessary to unlatch the receiver, remove it and expose the breech, then pull the hot barrel out with a metal claw or tab. As all parts were well heated this operation was rather delicate, and in the dark it was a nightmare.

The MG 34 became ubiquitous throughout the army,

being mounted on armoured vehicles as the coaxial gun and doubling as an anti-aircraft machine gun on other mounts. It served throughout the war, but it was a complicated weapon, it demanded a lot of factory effort to make, and it was sensitive to mud, dust and snow; so in 1942 it was replaced by the MG 42, probably the most famous machine gun of the entire war, though it was difficult to distinguish it from the 34 until one got very close. The MG 42 used a different system of barrel locking, though it stuck to the same method of operation, namely short recoil. The barrel changing was greatly improved and made so easy that a hot barrel could be taken out without ever needing to touch it. The rate of fire could be adjusted up to a maximum of nearly 1,300 rounds per minute. At this rate the individual shots almost merged into one continuous sound of tearing cloth, the gun heated rapidly, and its appetite for belts of ammunition was wonderful to see. But it was a frightening thing to

have bullets coming one's way in that quantity, and the sound of a 'Spandau', as it was always called, is still recalled by Allied veterans with a certain amount of dread. MG 34s and 42s were among the few items of German equipment which Allied soldiers were quite willing to capture and turn against their former owners.

But probably the best feature of the 42 was the manufacturing design, which owed something to that of the MP 40. The gun was intended from the very beginning to be made under wartime conditions, and it used the fewest possible machining processes and made the greatest possible use of stampings and pressings. Externally it had a very different finish from the MG 34, and the general feel was much less attractive, but it was far more resistant to dirt and rough treatment than the 34 and earned an enviable reputation in the Russian winter when most other weapons simply stopped working. In fact the design was so successful that it was revived in 1957 for the West German Army and is still serving under a new name and in the NATO calibre. It is otherwise exactly the same gun, now over 35 years old.

Firing these fast guns was an interesting experience for the newcomer. They were very difficult to hold steady, and they tended to walk away from the firer on the bipod. An assistant was a great help as he could guide the belt into the feedway and prevent it snatching and jerking. He was needed anyway to carry belts, and the normal three-man German gun team usually looked like a bunch of Mexican bandits as they habitually swathed themselves in ready-to-use belts. The 34 had a single-shot capability; the trigger rocked about its centre point, and pulling the upper half fired single shots, while the lower half operated as automatic. The 42 only fired automatic.

Precise production figures for these guns are not easy to find now, but the 34 probably topped 200,000 and more than 750,000 42s had been made by 1945. But the 34 and the 42

Left: An abandoned MG 42 machine gun overlooks a main road in Italy in October 1944; its crew has already been driven off by the Allied invaders.

Lehky Kulomet ZB 30		
Ammunition	7.92mm Gewehr Patrone 1898	
Length	45.75in	1161mm
Weight unloaded	21lb 5oz	9.60kg
Barrel	26.5in	672mm
Magazine	30-round detachable box	
Cyclic rate	500rpm	
Muzzle velocity	2500ft/sec	762m/sec

were not the only machine guns used in the Wermacht; by 1942 there was a general shortage of most infantry weapons and any serviceable equipment from the occupied countries was pressed into use. Czechoslovakia had always had a fine arms reputation and the factories either made German designs or continued turning out their own models. Thus the Czech ZB 30 was used in some numbers by the German Army; so was the earlier ZB 26 and at least two other designs from the same factory. Reserve units always get the thin end of the stick, and some German units were given a disheartening collection of foreign cast-offs – for instance in the Netherlands the captured Dutch guns were mounted along the Atlantic Wall, and among these were some venerable Schwarzloses and Maxims dating from long before World War I. But the front-line units were always properly looked after, and the German reputation for building fine machine guns and knowing how to use them was never higher than during World War II.

Anti-Tank Rifles

When the first British tanks rumbled over the trenches in 1916 there was no effective defence against them, but nine months later the German infantry had their first answer, a special anti-tank rifle. This was no more than an enlargement of the standard infantry Mauser, but it worked well enough for the remainder of that war.

The idea of anti-tank rifles was taken up by other countries during the post-war years, and when Germany came to re-arm the old Mauser was well out of date. In any case it had disappeared under the conditions of the Treaty of Versailles, so it was easy enough to start with a clean sheet and design something more up to date. Anti-tank rifles are by no means simple to produce, as there are so many conflicting features that have to be incorporated into the one weapon. It must be light enough to be carried by one man, or at most two, and yet it must penetrate the armour of the enemy's tanks. It must be small enough to conceal in a foxhole, yet it must have the greatest possible range so that tanks can be engaged before they have been spotted the gun position. Finally, it must have the highest possible rate of fire so that several shots can be got off in a short time, in case of a mass attack by armoured vehicles.

Faced with this requirement, some designers produced monstrosities, but in Germany the first thoughts were to use the lightest bullet possible and give it an extremely high muzzle velocity. This allowed a fairly light and compact weapon, yet the fast bullet offered reasonable penetration. The first design ultimately entered service in 1938 and is known as the Panzerbuchse 38. It used the old Mauser cartridge, which originally fired a 13mm bullet, necked down to take a special 7.92mm armour-piercing version using a tungsten carbide core. The PzB 38 was a fascinating weapon because it abandoned conventional rifle design and was very much a miniature artillery gun. It had a sliding-block breech instead of a bolt, and the barrel recoiled back along a short slide, camming the breech open as it did so. Fresh rounds were carried in a rack beside the breech and all that the gunner had to do was to move his hand a few inches from the butt and slip another round into the open breech; it thereupon clicked shut and was ready to fire again. It was one of the fastest and

Panzerbuchse Modell 39 (PzB 39)		
Ammunition	7.92mm/13mm anti-tank	
Length	62.25in	1581mm
Weight unloaded	27lb 4oz	12.35kg
Barrel	42.75in	1086mm
Magazine	Single shot	
Muzzle velocity	4150ft/sec	1265m/sec
Armour penetration	30mm at 100m at 30°	

neatest hand-operated infantry weapons ever made.

Unfortunately the PzB 38 was complicated to make, as with so many other pre-war weapons, and within a year a simplified version, the PzB 39, was on the stocks. One feature that had disappeared was the recoil slide, so that the jolt to the firer was greater and reloading slower. But it was a bit lighter, 27lb (12kg) instead of 35lb (16kg); even so it was a handful for one man.

These rifles were issued on a scale of one to a platoon and the PzB 38 was carried in the Polish campaign of 1939 and the Blitzkrieg of 1940, though in neither case was there any extensive use. However, it was already becoming clear that the tank builders were ahead of the game and anti-tank rifles were not really much use in stopping vehicles. This fact became painfully emphasized in Russia, where the rifles were quite useless and were generally thrown away by the exasperated and overloaded infantry. Some were modified with a cut-down barrel to shoot hollow-charge grenades, but the concept was hopeless, and once again the unfortunate weapons ended in roadside ditches. The Russian T-34 tank could shrug off this sort of attack, and the crew probably never even noticed what was happening.

In some desperation to give the infantry a means of defeating the Russian tanks yet another design was tried, this time much larger and heavier, in 20mm calibre. It was based on a pre-war Solothurn design, an ingenious and mechanically complicated self-loading rifle firing large, high-velocity solid shot, but it was already too late. The resulting PzB 41 had been derived partly from an aircraft cannon, so there must have been some common parts, which would have helped manufacture, but even so it was most expensive to make and difficult to maintain. The 20mm shot had a steel core (tungsten carbide was already extremely scarce), and it only penetrated 30mm of armour at 240m; this was quite inadequate for the Eastern Front and most of the production was sent to Italy where the rifle had some success against the Sherman tank's thinner armour.

As with so many German weapons, the anti-tank rifles showed remarkable design flair and are among the most interesting infantry equipment produced in the war. The pity is that the German High Command did not realize sooner that the day of the man-carried armour-piercing rifle was over before the war started, so that valuable effort could have been put to finding better ways of stopping tanks.

Panzerbuchse MSS 41 (Czech design)		
Ammunition	7.92mm special high velocity	
Length	47in	1195mm
Weight unloaded	40lb	18.14kg
Barrel	33in	839mm
Magazine	10-round detachable box	
Muzzle velocity	4000ft/sec	1219m/sec
Armour penetration	Not known	

ITALY

Italy has a long history of manufacturing arms and armour, dating back to the Middle Ages. The workshops of Brescia and Turin enjoyed a reputation for swords, daggers, edged weapons and protective armour for hundreds of years, and with the introduction of firearms they turned their skills to making guns of exceptional quality and beauty. With the coming of the internal combustion engine the workshops boomed even more, and since the start of the century Italian cars and engines have shown an efficiency and quality that has been the envy of others. In aircraft, and particularly in aircraft engines, the Italian designs were always among the leaders, as their performance in the international air races of the 1920s and 1930s shows. Throughout the time that the British were wrestling for the Schneider Trophy, it was an Italian Macchi which was just behind, and only behind by a very small margin.

In view of this excellent background it is all the more surprising to find that the Italian small arms in both world wars were so poor, and it is hard to find the real reason. On the one hand there appears to have been a dearth of designers, and in machine guns particularly the Government seemed to rely entirely on one man, Revelli, who was by no means exceptional. When Breda produced their own light machine gun they too took an unfortunate idea, and somehow never seemed to be able to get away from it. The Mannlicher-Carcano rifle was no worse than any other when it was brought out in 1891, but it was screaming out for improvement in 1918, and it never got it. Only in the modern weapons were there signs of some originality and good sense in the design. The Beretta pistols were excellent; the Beretta submachine guns, while somewhat heavy, were among the best made in the whole war, and they enjoyed a reputation shared with few others. Beretta showed that it could be done when necessary, but this ability was entirely confined to the one firm, and it may be that their strong commercial instincts were the driving force that led to it.

At all times there was a grave lack of factory capacity available for small arms. The fact was that in the middle 1930s Italy did not have the manufacturing base to support a modern war, and in order to equip and supply her armies properly she needed to call on outside sources. Pride forbade this, and anyway such sources were simply not to be had at that time. All Europe was re-arming and industry in every country was going full blast on its own national programmes. Finally, Italy was not rich; the Depression had damaged the economy and its recovery took longer than with some other countries. The grandiose schemes of re-building and colonizing, particularly on the North African coast, together with the Abyssinian War, also took their toll of the available money. There were too few new factories and too little new investment, and it was all reflected in the war material.

It seems likely that at no time was the Italian Army ever equipped with its full complement of weapons and ammunition. The élite units always were, and great efforts were made to keep the battalions in North Africa up to scale, but this was not enough. When the Expeditionary Corps was formed to go to Russia and help the Wehrmacht in 1941 there were serious shortages. Despite the best efforts of the logisticians, the infantry platoons had in many cases only one light machine gun instead of three; the medium machine guns were well below scale, and in some battalions non-existent. The anti-tank guns were few and far between and submachine guns were down to one per platoon. It was not a good start for a major campaign, and the troops suffered because of it.

But if any indication is needed of the arms supply, it can be best shown by the ammunition position. In 1891 the calibre chosen was 6.5mm, and the cartridge was quite typical of its day, with a round-nosed bullet of modest power. Most nations changed to the pointed 'spitzer' bullet in about 1908,

but not Italy, and the round-nosed bullet survived until 1945. The trouble with this bullet was that it quickly lost velocity and thus striking power after it left the muzzle, and so the effective range was shorter than all others. Also it was not particularly good in machine guns. It should have been changed in 1918, but it wasn't. At last, in 1937, its deficiencies were realized and a new bullet produced in a slightly larger calibre. This was a half-way improvement, 20 years too late, and there was no time to convert all the weapons before the war started. In fact, to even think of trying to change the calibre of the entire national armoury with the resources available and the desperately short time left was in itself a minor attack of madness, and sure enough it all went wrong. At the same time the Italian Army was taking into service some machine guns which fired different ammunition from 6.5mm, and which required separate manufacture and separate supply, and also authorizing the issue of pistols and submachine guns which had different calibres and types of round. In the end it seems that the Italian Army went to war with no less than four different rounds of ammunition for rifles and machine guns and four more different types of pistols and submachine guns. How the supply organization coped is a mystery.

Looking back now, it is easy to be critical and to point to the obvious areas of weakness. No doubt they were much more difficult to detect at the time, though some, such as the variety of ammunition types, must have been glaringly obvious. The one failing which seems to be common to the entire control of the Italian armaments for the infantry, and in many cases for the army as a whole, is the lack of a proper coherent policy which was followed through. One can see clear signs of hurried arrangements to patch up as each crisis was reached, but little evidence exists of any long-term planning. A steady programme of re-barrelling the rifles and machine guns could have been carried out at quite a slow pace from about 1930 onwards, with minimal strain on the factories, and by 1940 the 6.5mm round would have been no more than a memory, but to try and do it in a couple of years with war clouds hanging over every horizon was crazy. But this sort of philosophy is of little value now. The main thing is that the Italian soldier was sent to war with too little equipment, and what he had was of less than adequate capability. It is to his credit that he fought as well as he did with it.

Below : Italian troops, armed with Carcano rifles, parade before Mussolini and the royal family.

Pistols

The Italian Army used quite large numbers of pistols, mainly because they were the standard armament of all officers, several vehicle drivers, most crews of armoured vehicles, and some NCOs. In addition the Italian Navy and Air Force used them. The naval officers and petty officers carried pistols, and so did aircrews of most fighting planes. The numbers required were very substantial, and it is no surprise that there was more than one type in general issue. In fact, it was necessary to buy in stocks of civilian models since the factories could not make sufficient of the approved patterns. The picture of the World War II pistols is therefore one of some variety and wide distribution.

The oldest pistol which was officially in service was the Glisenti automatic which dated back to 1910 and which had seen extensive use in World War I. In fact it was patented in 1906, but some manufacture was undertaken by Metallurgica Bresciana Temprini and their output went under the name of Brixia. The two names have led to some understandable confusion in the minds of historians, and the Italian Army on several occasions indicated that it was taking a neutral position by referring to the weapon as the Brixia-Glisenti. Certainly the majority of the production was by the firm of Glisenti, who also designed the cartridge. Further than that

it is scarcely worth delving, since the point at issue is the weapon and not its precise origins.

As an automatic the Glisenti Model 10 1910 was a workmanlike and interesting design. In appearance it resembles the German Parabellum, though the internal mechanism may well owe more to the early Mauser designs, since there is no sign of the toggle-joint lock of the Parabellum. The calibre was 9mm, but the round was a special 9mm of slightly smaller overall length than the Parabellum, and of 25% less power. The differences in length were not so great that one type could not be loaded into the other pistol, and this was a potential hazard, as will be explained. However, the bullet of the Glisenti was more pointed than any other, so a mistaken loading had to be more deliberate than accidental.

The locking system which was used was typical of the time of its invention. Today we would describe it as a semi-locked breech rather than a full lock, and it worked by a rotating catch which was held by a strong flat spring in the butt. This catch was rotated fully forward when the breech was closed, and it projected through the long barrel extension into the square bolt, where it was held in a recess. As the cartridge fired, both barrel and bolt recoiled together, turning the catch backwards until it was pushed out of engagement with the bolt, whereupon this part continued to recoil for its full length of travel. The barrel was stopped at this point and then returned to battery by its own separate

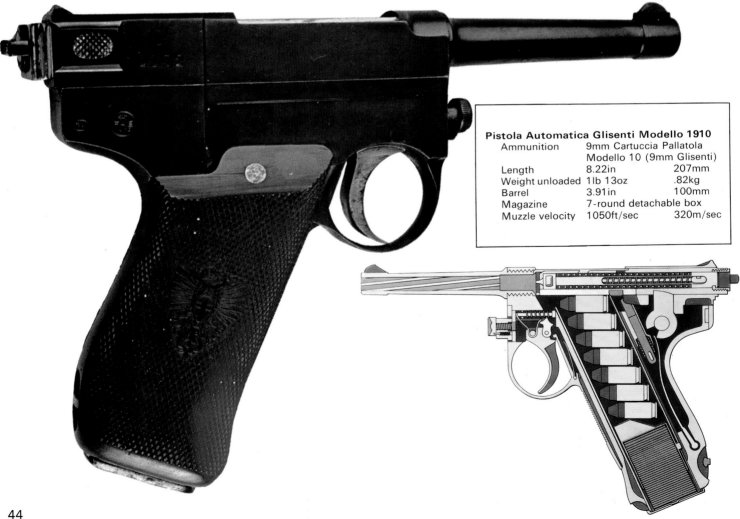

Pistola Automatica Glisenti Modello 1910

Ammunition	9mm Cartuccia Pallatola Modello 10 (9mm Glisenti)	
Length	8.22in	207mm
Weight unloaded	1lb 13oz	.82kg
Barrel	3.91in	100mm
Magazine	7-round detachable box	
Muzzle velocity	1050ft/sec	320m/sec

spring. The locking catch made sure that the barrel and bolt were not able to move relative to each other until the rearward movement had been sufficient to allow the pressures in the barrel to drop to a safe level, but there were snags to this arrangement. In fact, the lock was not fully positive, and as soon as the rear movement began, so did the unlocking, since the catch stayed still and the moving parts rotated it as they recoiled. This meant that if a more powerful cartridge were fired, either by accident or intentionally, then the bolt would be unlocking while the pressure was higher than the designer intended. What is more, the barrel and bolt would fly back much faster than was intended, and the stops for both would be strained by the impact.

The danger which was brought about by more powerful ammunition was probably less real than this account might give one to believe, since the pistol was always issued with its own ammunition, and at the time of its design there were in any case dozens of different types of pistol ammunition in existence. It was perfectly normal to make pistols and ammunition to match with no regard for other versions in other countries. With the Glisenti ammunition the pistol was perfectly safe and most reliable. The lower power did mean that there was some loss of performance when compared with other types, but this was not enough to cause much trouble at the ranges at which pistols were used.

There were one or two other peculiarities about the Glisenti which are worth recording. It had most of the left side of the frame cut away and covered with a light metal plate. This was good for cleaning but not for strength, and it had a habit of shaking itself loose during firing. There was a grip safety, which was an advanced idea for 1910, but it was on the front of the grip, which is a little less convenient for the hand, and it only worked on the trigger, which is not particularly safe, since it means that the action can be cocked and not held at all. An accidental jolt could allow the hammer to fire although the trigger was held.

These considerations apart, the Glisenti served the Italian Army well for about 35 years, though in World War II it was regarded as a second-line issue and only a few of them appeared among the front-line infantry units. They were carried by the Carabinieri and by reserve troops, and some were issued to the Italian Navy to supplement their stocks.

The Glisenti was actually supposed to have been replaced during World War I by the first of the military Berettas, this time the 1916 model, and some of these survived through the next war, being given to aircrew for the most part. The 1916 Beretta was a small pistol made to an old design which was by no means modern in World War I, but the exigencies of war pressed it into use. It was originally meant as a 7.65mm civilian automatic, operating by simple blowback, and it could be re-barrelled for the 9mm short cartridge also. By fitting a stronger recoil spring it was made to fire the Glisenti 9mm, which gave it a fairly severe recoil and kick, but it also introduced the possibility of loading the Parabellum cartridge. Straight away the safety limits were over-reached and the firing reaction was most unpleasant. Some thousands of these little pistols, more or less worn, were still being used in 1945. One oddity about them, which instantly distinguishes the 7.65mm models, though it does not appear on the 9mm ones, is the ejector. On the smaller calibres the empty case was pushed off the face of the bolt by the firing pin, which poked out to its full extent at the end of recoil. This threw the empty case straight upwards. The 9mm versions used a conventional lever.

Pistola Automatica Beretta Modello 1934		
Ammunition	7.65mm automatic pistol, 9mm short	
Length	6in	152mm
Weight unloaded	1lb 7.5oz	.66kg
Barrel	3.75in	94mm
Magazine	7-round detachable box	
Muzzle velocity	825ft/sec	251m/sec

Below: An officer of the Alpini takes aim with his Beretta Model 1934 pistol.

Following the 1916 model there were several Berettas which were produced primarily for commercial sales, but of course the firm always had its eyes on the chance of Government orders and to this end it improved the 1915 model and made it in the 9mm Glisenti calibre as the Model of 1922, then of 1923, and then of 1931. This last one was adopted by the Italian Navy, though in 7.65mm calibre. The army took some, but not many, and most of those which still survive have the anchor symbol and the letters RM (Regia Marina d'Italia) in a brass button on the grips. Apart from improved lockwork and quite outstanding excellence of finish the 1931 model is little changed from those which went before it, except that it had a feature which became a hallmark of the later versions. This was a small spur on the bottom plate of the magazine, to prevent a large hand from slipping off the grips. All these Berettas were quite small and the length of the butt on all models was shorter than with many other designs. This short length also meant that the magazines held fewer rounds, seven being normal.

The 1934 Beretta was the final design, and proof of its worth is the fact that the design is still made and sold commercially today. This pistol was originally made in 7.65mm but after about 1938 manufacture seems to have turned entirely to 9mm short, and this is the pistol which was used most during the war. It is relatively small, quite light at 1lb 7oz (0.62kg), and easily carried. It became the standard side-arm of the Italian Army and was carried by all the front-line units of infantry, Bersaglieri and Alpini. Although thought to be rather less powerful than a military pistol really warranted, the Beretta was enormously popular and showed itself to be reliable and trouble-free. Much of this freedom from trouble may have stemmed from the good standard of manufacture, but the design had been refined by 1934, and there were few errors in it. After 1943 the Germans took over the Beretta factories and demanded such a high output that the standards of the weapons began to decline, and pistols made from then on until the end of the war show a marked deterioration in quality.

There is one other Beretta model, that of 1935, and this differed from the others only in that it had a lighter slide. It was therefore issued to the Italian Air Force, but apart from the lightening of the slide it is no different from the standard 1934 pattern. One wonders quite why it was thought so necessary to reduce the weight, for it must have meant difficulties in the factory with yet one more variant to be made and tested.

One of the features of the Beretta family – and it appeared in all of them from 1915 onwards – was the fact that when the last round in the magazine was fired the platform came up and jammed the working parts to the rear. The empty magazine was then quite hard to pull out, as it was held by the platform, and as soon as it was free the slide shut. On putting in a fresh magazine the slide had to be cocked again. It was an unnecessary and sometimes annoying movement, and it could easily have been avoided by fitting a separate holding-open catch.

Hand-Operated Rifles

Like so many other countries in 1939, Italy armed its soldiers with an old design of bolt-action rifle, but the trouble with the Italian one was that it was older and less satisfactory than most and it should have been replaced after World War I. When the first smokeless powders were making the old large-bore rifles obsolete, Italy set up a commission to investigate a suitable rifle for the army. The result was the 1891 Mannlicher-Parravicino-Carcano, a fairly straightforward bolt-action rifle with a Mannlicher-type magazine, a Mauser-type bolt action and some local improvements. The point about the Mannlicher magazine is that it depends for its operation on the ammunition being loaded in a clip or charger which remains in the magazine until the last round has been used, when it falls out through a hole in the bottom. Usually, the Mannlicher chargers take six rounds, and this insufficient supply was retained until the end of the war since there was no way of altering it. One cannot just enlarge a Mannlicher system to take two chargers; it won't work.

Above: Detail of the Mannlicher-Carcano 1891, showing the method of loading the six-round charger.

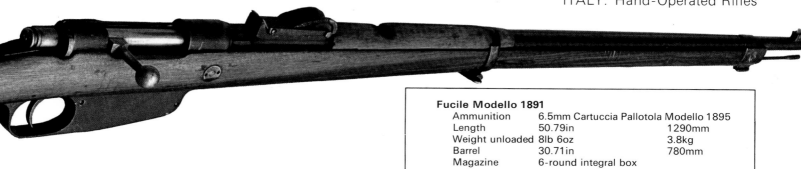

Fucile Modello 1891		
Ammunition	6.5mm Cartuccia Pallotola Modello 1895	
Length	50.79in	1290mm
Weight unloaded	8lb 6oz	3.8kg
Barrel	30.71in	780mm
Magazine	6-round integral box	
Muzzle velocity	2400ft/sec	730m/sec

Fucile Modello 1891/38		
Ammunition	6.5mm Cartuccia Pallotola Modello 1895	
Length	40in	1016mm
Weight unloaded	7lb 8oz	3.09kg
Barrel	21.25in	540mm
Magazine	5-round integral box	
Muzzle velocity	2483ft/sec	814m/sec

Another feature of the first Carcanos was the rifling, which for some special reason increased its twist between the breech and the muzzle, a refinement no other country found it worthwhile to include. But the main feature of the Carcano was the round that it used. The 6.5mm was adequate enough in 1891, but well down the scale by 1918. In the Abyssinian campaign of 1934 there were many complaints about the lack of carrying power and general poor ballistics of the 6.5mm, both in rifles and in machine guns. In 1937 steps were taken to produce a new round with a better performance, although at no great cost, since money was scarce. The result was really a redesigned bullet in the same case. The calibre went up to 7.35mm, a most unusual size, and the weight of the bullet went down a bit. It was more pointed at the nose and the weight was kept down by using an aluminium tip, which also meant that it rapidly became unstable if it hit anything and tumbled, causing far more damage than if it had kept straight. This gave it a distinctly dubious reputation, but luckily there was nowhere near enough time left to change all the rifles in the army to the new calibre. After trying for two years to get some sort of mass-production renovation line started the Government had to stop – and not only stop but

actually back-pedal and take some converted rifles back to the factory and once more make them into 6.5mm. But of course not all of them went back, and in 1940 there were no less than nine separate and identifiable variants in service, using the two different types of ammunition.

After all these contortions it is a wonder that any unit went to war in one piece at all. The production of 7.35mm ammunition had to be stopped after a few months in order to keep up the supply of the other types, and this meant that a number of badly needed rifles were left sitting in store because there was no ammunition for them. Most of them were sold off as collectors' pieces after 1945. In Israel and Syria they were re-barrelled into 7.92mm Mauser calibre, a risky procedure since the bolt was not meant for the pressure. In the USA a 7.35mm re-barrelled back to 6.5mm in 1939 was sold to a man in Texas who took it into a high building and shot President Kennedy with it, proving that the 6.5mm round was lethal enough if used correctly. Others were used for police and reserve units.

Some of the Carcanos were designated TS, meaning for Special Troops. This did not mean special troops in the now accepted sense of the word, it meant line-of-communication troops, drivers, and gunners, men who used a rifle as a last resort. For these the rifle was shortened to a carbine and a short folding knife-bayonet was attached at the muzzle; the infantry carried their bayonets separately in scabbards. But the really strange feature of the Carcano was the way it fired grenades. By 1939 practically every nation in the world had some way of launching grenades from rifles, all using some sort of muzzle cup or spigot. Not the Carcano! It had a small mortar bolted to the side. This extraordinary device was a short-barrelled smooth-bore gun with a similar breech to the rifle which took a ballistite cartridge. To load it, the bolt of

Above: A cutaway view of the Mannlicher-Carcano 1891 with the charger in place, ready for firing.

the rifle had to be removed and put in the launcher breech, then a cartridge could be loaded, a bomb popped down the muzzle, and the rifle stood with its butt on the ground. Now the launcher trigger could be pulled, and away went a grenade, to no more distance than if it had been put on the muzzle as with every other rifle. This strange method of launching meant that the Carcano grenadier had to carry practically double the weight of the actual rifle and perform a quick bolt-swapping trick every time he wished to fire the thing, leaving himself defenceless as he did so.

Submachine Guns

Italy shares the distinction with Germany of first developing the submachine gun as an infantry weapon, using the twin-barrelled Villar Perosa in 1915. From these beginnings there sprang a family of submachine guns of great merit, all of them made by Beretta and all of them every bit as good as any other made in the world.

The first of these weapons appeared in 1918 as the Moschetto Automatico Beretta Modello 1918, and frequently known as either the Beretta '18 or the MAB 18. It was designed by Tullio Marengoni, who was to carry on and be the guiding spirit behind all the Beretta submachine guns that followed in the next 30 years. In this first one he showed the skill and attention to detail that soon became his trademark. The gun actually used the mechanism of the Villar Perosa, mounted in a wooden stock closely modelled on the then current Mannlicher-Carcano carbine and capable of accepting the same bayonet. Because it had the VP mechanism the MAB 18 had a vertical magazine feeding downwards, a distinction which it shared only with the Owen gun from Australia.

The MAB 18 was chambered for the 1910 Glisenti pistol round, which was entirely sensible, but the excessive rate of fire of the VP was unfortunately still present. A feature of the MAB 18 which was to recur on other versions was the use of two triggers, the front one firing single shots, the rear one fully automatic. This was a simple and reliable way of introducing the two modes of fire, allowing the minimum of complication internally, but adding to the weight by a little. Once the firer gets used to using two triggers it is probably the most satisfactory way of selecting fire that there is, and certainly it is easier to learn than the selector levers which some guns have been given. The Model 18 was never made in large numbers, but it stayed in service with some sections of the Italian Army and the police until 1945. It was used in the North African desert until 1941, when it was largely withdrawn and was replaced by the Model 1938, but it was re-issued in Italy to reserve units.

There were at least two variants of the Model 18. One was a single-shot police weapon with a folding bayonet and the other a 1930 model which attempted to up-date the design for the least expense and trouble. It fitted the same two triggers and general mechanism but put the magazine under-neath, where it was less in the way, and used the more powerful Parabellum round, which of course meant fitting stronger springs. It again saw limited war service, though mostly in Italy itself.

These variations on a design of World War I were only stop-gaps which sufficed during the rather lean years of comparative peace after 1918. The Italian campaigns in Africa made few demands on submachine guns, but the Spanish Civil War brought the need into sharp relief and Italy began to design a modern gun in keeping with those beginning to appear in other European countries. Once again it was Beretta who took the lead, and in 1938 the first of what was to become a long series was offered to the military. The Model 1938 was very much on the same lines as many other guns, and there is a strong likelihood that the 1934 Bergmann was used as the basis for the design. The general outline was that of a great many similar guns of that era, a one-piece wooden stock, a machined body, and a longish barrel covered with a sheet steel jacket perforated for cooling.

The amount of machining required in manufacture was normal by the standards of the day, and excessive by today's. The barrel was quite long, and all parts were robust and extremely well made. The magazine fed upwards from below the body, and came in a variety of sizes holding from 10 to 40 rounds. The calibre was 9mm Parabellum, and there were again two triggers. By this time the two triggers were becoming a Beretta trademark, as was the standard of finish. The overall length was only a little short of that of the

Moschetto Automatico Modello 1938A		
Ammunition	9mm Cartuccia Pallotola Modello 38A	
Length	37.5in	953mm
Weight unloaded	9lb 4oz	4.19kg
Barrel	12.5in	318mm
Magazine	10-, 20-, 30- or 40-round detachable box	
Cyclic rate	600rpm	
Muzzle velocity	1370ft/sec	417m/sec

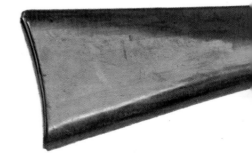

Mannlicher-Carcano carbine, and the weight roughly similar. Another Beretta speciality was the method of cocking by a separate bolt handle, which was not attached to the bolt, and after cocking was pushed forward where it stayed throughout firing. The magazine opening could be closed off with a small sliding plate when the gun was being carried without a magazine fitted, and another refinement was the separate firing pin. The pin was cammed forward and backward at the end of the firing stroke of the bolt, using a pivoted cam on the underside of the bolt – a most complicated and expensive arrangement.

This gun was issued to the army, police and Carabinieri in small numbers and the factory was able to keep pace with the demand. In addition to filling the need of the Italian Army, the factory also managed to cope with export orders from Germany and Rumania, though the latter was not very large. Later, the Germans were asking for all that could be made, and the factory was working at full blast.

Some small modifications were introduced in late 1938, but the basic weapon stayed more or less as it had been designed until 1942. By then it had become apparent that the quantities had to be increased dramatically, and the 1938 design was not going to be capable of being made in sufficient numbers as it stood. The methods of manufacture were changed drastically, and to some extent so was the design. The basic trigger, mechanism, magazine and general assembly were retained, but the machined components were replaced by stampings or pressings wherever possible. The sheet-steel

Above: Italian partisans armed with a Beretta 38A and (left) a British Sten gun.

Pistola Mitragliatrice Beretta Modello 1938/42

Ammunition	9mm Parabellum	
Length	31.5in	800mm
Weight unloaded	7lb 3oz	3.26kg
Barrel	8.5in	216mm
Magazine	20- or 40-round detachable box	
Cyclic rate	550rpm	
Muzzle velocity	1250ft/sec	381m/sec

barrel-jacket disappeared, and the plain barrel had a compensator put into the muzzle. The bolt was simplified and given a fixed firing pin and the wooden forestock was cut back until it only reached to the magazine. Even so the gun was recognizably a Beretta, and still very much like the Model 38. It was known as the Model 1938/42, and in this guise could be turned out in large numbers.

The experiences in the North African desert had convinced the Italian Army that it needed more firepower, and this was reinforced in the fighting in Sicily, so submachine guns began to become more frequent in infantry battalions and were issued down to section NCOs. They also became a useful weapon for partisans and special forces as well as the crews of some armoured vehicles. Berettas were used on all the battle fronts where the Italian Army was operating. The majority of the production up to 1942 went to the desert and were used in the well-known battles that ebbed and flowed along the northern coast, but many were lost there too, hence the increased production with the 38/42. The partisans in Italy carried them in quite large numbers, and it seems likely that Mussolini was shot with a 38/42 wielded by a partisan.

After 1943 the German Army took the entire output of the factory for its own forces, but production never stopped, and the gun was still in service when the war ended and for at least ten years after that. Later models are still to be found in a variety of countries, proving that the initial design was both sound and practical.

Apart from the basic 1938 model Beretta there was almost no other submachine gun in Italy during the war. Two different types got some way towards production. The first was the Beretta Model I, a somewhat confusing name since it appeared in 1941 while the Model 38 was still on the production line. The Model I was a much lightened and streamlined gun obviously owing something to the German MP 38 in that it had much the same folding stock and a roughly similar outline. It was intended for paratroops, but only small quantities were made and its place in the factory was taken by the 38/42. The Model I appears to have had the same simplified barrel and bolt as the 38/42, so perhaps the latter gained from the design work on the former.

The next gun actually got into limited production, though probably no more than 6,000 were made. This was the TZ-45, the brainchild of Messrs Toni and Zorzoli, who allegedly designed it in 1944 and put it into production in 1945. It was a very simple and rather crudely made gun, looking a bit like a thinned-out version of a Sten with a longer barrel. It had a telescoping wire butt and used the Beretta magazine. Its virtue lay in the fact that it had two separate safety features, which was most unusual at that time. One was a conventional change lever, which could also lock the bolt; the second was a grip safety just behind the magazine, where the forward hand holds the gun. The TZ-45 may well have been the first gun to use such a device. But 1945 was no time to be introducing new submachine guns, and the design faded away after a little licensed production in Burma, of all

places, in the late 1940s.

The final Italian gun is something of a mystery, although several are known to exist. The FNAB was developed and produced in Brescia in 1943 by the Fabbrica Nazionale d'Arme, who are said to have made 7,000. These were used by the Italian and German forces. If this is true one wonders who authorized the venture, since the FNAB must have taken at least twice as long to make as the Beretta, and factory time was not exactly free at that time in the war. However, it *was* made, and perhaps it did reach 7,000. It was an extremely complex and well-built gun, utilizing costly and slow machine methods and fitted with a three-part bolt with a form of retarder to the blowback action. It fired from a closed bolt, which is almost unique in submachine guns, and as a result had to have a separate firing pin. Some ingenuity went into ensuring that there was a short hesitation before each round was fired. This action combined with the retarded bolt gave a rate of fire of 400 rpm, which meant that the gun was easily controllable when on full automatic, but it had a change lever for single shot also. All told it was a triumph of Italian craftsmanship, but it was scarcely a weapon of war. What it actually cost to make one shudders to think; perhaps it is as well for the Italian economy that production ceased at the mystic 7,000.

Machine Guns

In many respects the philosophy of the use of machine guns in the Italian Army was much the same as in Britain. The infantry section was based on a light machine gun, capable of being carried and operated by one man but always given a two-man team, and fed by a magazine. This was backed up by a support machine gun, or medium gun as it was called in Britain, which was deployed by the company commander, or in many cases held centrally at battalion HQ. These guns were tripod-mounted, belt-fed, sustained-fire guns capable of giving prolonged supporting fire with considerable accuracy over the maximum range of the ammunition. They were capable of being carried in pieces by their three- or four-man crews, but were frequently given a small vehicle.

The standard light machine gun in the Italian Army during the war was the Breda Model 30, a gun which was the result of ten years of development and alteration. The Società Italiana Ernesto Breda used to be a locomotive works in Brescia. During World War I it was turned over to the manufacture of small arms, building the water-cooled Revelli as a sub-contractor from Fiat. After the armistice, Breda found themselves with a factory tooled-up for small arms and no chance of getting back into the locomotive business, so they tried for an attractive contract that the Government was offering for a home-designed light machine gun. The result was the 1924 model, which was slightly improved two years later when it actually got the coveted contract. Two thousand guns were made, and the firm flourished so well that in 1930 the patents and plant of the Fiat factory were bought up and the latest model was brought out.

The Breda 1930 model was little changed from the 1924, except in detail, and it remained unchanged until 1945. This was a mistake, for it was a gun that cried out for improvement from the day of its birth. One hopes for the sake of the Italian public that Breda produced better locomotives than they did machine guns. No doubt many of the Italian infantry who had to use the guns would agree, and add that it was a pity that Breda strayed into the gun world at all, for the Model 30 was a positive wasp's nest of troubles.

There is an old maxim in engineering that what looks right generally is right; the Breda looks wrong, and it mostly is wrong. It was an ungainly gun which looked exactly as if all its component parts had been added to each other, one after the other. There was no cohesion or smoothness about the outline. In the middle was a rectangular block; in front of that the barrel lay in a trough; beside it the magazine swung forward and back; behind it was a cylindrical extension to the body, carrying the backsight and cocking handle, and on

Below: Alpini troops on the Greco-Albanian front, armed with a Breda Model 30 machine gun. This particular weapon was very susceptible to dirt and snow, both because of the many slots in the design and because of the oiling of the cartridge cases before chambering. The Breda Model 30 machine gun was issued throughout the Italian Army on all battle fronts. It acquired a bad reputation for reliability and was abandoned after the war.

the far end of this extension the butt and pistol grip were hung. Everything was angular and apparently open to the air; there were slots and holes all over; it looked, and it was, a perfect dust and dirt trap.

This unhappy little gun had a variety of unusual features. The first was the method of operation, which was by delayed blowback using what is technically known as the Stange method of locking, which can be most easily described as a locking collar around the breech and bolt head. The bolt had lugs on its head, and the breech had a loose collar around it which was free to rotate, but could not move back off the barrel. The bolt head fitted into the collar, and then if the collar was given a slight twist to the right or left the bolt was firmly locked onto the breech. When the gun was fired the barrel and bolt recoiled back for a short distance, hence the trough in front of the body – it allowed the barrel to move while still supporting it. After a short distance the collar was twisted by a stud and the bolt released, flying back under the remaining pressure in the barrel to act in the normal blowback fashion. On the return forward it pushed the barrel back into place and locked the collar again.

There are snags to this apparently simple system. One is the fact that the cartridge case is jerked out of the breech without any preliminary easing, and unless a case is gently levered out for the first few thousandths of an inch there is a

Breda Modello 1930

Ammunition	6.5mm Cartuccia Pallotola Modello M95	
Length	48.4in	1230mm
Weight unloaded	22lb 8oz	10.2kg
Barrel	20.5in	520mm
Magazine	20-round box	
Cyclic rate	475rpm	
Muzzle velocity	200ft/sec	609m/sec

distinct danger of its breaking off at the base, since the walls of the case are tight against the sides of the chamber. So it was with the Breda, and the designer had to resort to oiling the cases; this was done by a small reservoir on top of the body with a pump which gave each case a short spray of oil as it was fed towards the chamber. As a result the inside of the gun was always well lubricated – too well lubricated – and attracted dust and dirt like a magnet. The cases often picked up grit as well as oil, and so they acted as small grindstones as they moved to and fro. This did little for reliability, and often led to the cases jamming in the breech just as much as if they had never been oiled at all. In the desert the gunners had a miserable time cleaning the sticky sand mixture from the bolt.

One of the difficulties with all the early magazine-fed light machine guns had been finding a suitable magazine. The Breda designer decided that the best solution was to make his on substantial lines and attach it to the gun, filling it with a large charger. The magazine was placed on the right of the gun and hinged forward to lie alongside the barrel. To load, the gunner took a charger of 20 rounds and pushed it into the magazine, pulled out the empty charger and snapped the now-filled magazine back into the feedway. The advantage to this system is the fact that the well-made magazine is less likely to suffer stoppages from damaged lips or bent sides, and the gun can use ammunition taken from the riflemen in the section if necessary. The disadvantages are rather less obvious. One is that the magazine does still get damaged because it sticks out from the side all the time. The next is that by putting it on the right of the gun to help the gunner load, it is really on the wrong side for tactical use, though it is probably better for carrying. Finally, to clean the magazine the gun has to stop firing altogether, and reloading by pushing in chargers is never as fast as changing full magazines.

Just to finish off on the unfortunate Breda, it had no carrying handle, so the wretched gunner was forced to pick up a hot gun in his arms whenever he had to move. Though

the barrel could easily be changed if it overheated, the sights were on the body of the gun, so changing barrels was bound to lead to a loss of accuracy. Despite all these troubles the Breda was issued throughout the army and used on all the battle fronts. In North Africa the combination of the low-powered 6.5mm round and the amount of dust and sand gave it a bad reputation for reliability and it was dropped after the war with almost indecent haste.

The arrangements for the provision of a support machine gun to the infantry were in some disarray when Italy went to war in 1940. There were substantial numbers of the 1914 Fiat-Revelli still in service, but this was already obsolete and efforts to replace had not been entirely successful. In fact there were three or four different guns to choose from, and at least three different calibres of ammunition too. Picking one's way through this tangle is not easy.

The doyen of the group was the 1914 Model Fiat-Revelli, designed by Revelli and built by Fiat, who, it will be remembered, gave Breda substantial sub-contracts. The 1914 Revelli was a remarkable gun by any standards, and certainly did not live up to the reputation normally associated with the Italian arms industry, but the blame can perhaps best be laid with Revelli, and the administration which accepted his ideas. Although it looked much like the Maxim and Browning designs which the other nations used, the Revelli was markedly different, and one would be mistaken in assuming that it could perform to the same standards. It was water-

cooled and mounted on a tripod, in which it resembled the Maxims, but it was unique among medium machine guns in having a magazine feed, and no ordinary magazine either. It was a box holding 50 rounds in ten columns of five each, the arrangement being not unlike ten rifle magazines laid alongside each other, with their separate platforms and springs, but with only a thin partition between each. The box fed in from the left side below the bolt, and as the bolt went forward it took a round from the top of a column in exactly the same way as a rifle. When five rounds were fired a catch tripped and the box indexed across to present the next column of five to the bolt, and so on until all 50 had been fired, when the empty box was pushed out of the right side, and the feed was ready to accept another. This unusual magazine could be loaded with loose rounds taken from nearby riflemen if need be, and it was thought that this, together with the relatively small size of the box, was an advantage, but in action it was found that there was rarely

time to reload. And alas, the boxes were easily damaged and bent.

Apart from the magazine feed, the Revelli showed a few other strange ideas. The mechanism worked by delayed blowback, using the same delay device as on the Glisenti pistol, which is a swinging wedge rotating on a pin in the body. The barrel and bolt were allowed to recoil a short distance together until the wedge turned out of engagement, whereupon the bolt carried on under normal blowback action. As with so many blowback systems, this one suffered from difficulties in extracting the case suddenly without a preliminary easing movement. Revelli overcame this by fitting the first of the notorious oiling systems, with its associated pump and spray. As with the Breda, the oil collected grit and dirt and jammed the mechanism, while the complicated magazine arrangements added their own troubles.

An oddity of the gun was the bolt, which ran along the top of the body and stuck out at the back in the form of a cocking handle. This handle moved with the bolt, and at the extreme of backward travel met a buffer just in front of the gunner's firing handles, so that throughout firing it hammered away about two inches from his fingers, entirely in the open, and busily pulling more dirt into the mechanism. It made for great concentration on the part of gunners during night shoots, and led to a certain nervousness about clearing stoppages.

Fiat-Revelli Modello 1914

Ammunition	6.5mm Cartuccia Pallotola Modello M95	
Length	46.5in	1180mm
Weight unloaded	371lb 8oz	17kg
Barrel	25.75in	654mm
Magazine	50-round strip-feed box	
Cyclic rate	400rpm	
Muzzle velocity	2100ft/sec	640m/sec

This elderly gun fired at the modest rate of 400 rpm, which was a small return for its weight and complication, and not surprisingly some effort was directed towards finding an improvement as soon as World War I ended. It took no less than 15 years to produce it, and when it came there must have been many who wondered whether the wait had been worthwhile.

The 1935 replacement for the Revelli was nevertheless still a Revelli and little more than a rehash of the 1914 model – in fact, many of the ones issued were actually 1914 guns with the 1935 modifications incorporated, a sad reflection on the state of the art in Italy at that time. The delayed blowback was retained, in spite of the fact that it was known that it needed some form of lubrication in the chamber to release the fired case. Revelli allowed for this by fluting the chamber, the idea being to let some gas leak round the outside and balance some of the internal pressure so that the case was, in effect, floating in the chamber. Such a theory is fine in chambers using ammunition designed for the process. The updated 1935 models didn't do so; they had an 8mm round with improved ballistics over the 6.5mm, but there were improved pressures also and the fluting only functioned at slow rates of fire.

When the barrel and chamber got well warmed all the old troubles appeared again, and there was nothing for it but to go back to oiling. So guns were called back from service and fitted with the old 1914-pattern oil tanks and pumps, but there were not enough to go round, so another expedient was thought up. Ammunition was oiled before it was loaded into the magazines, which was a policy of disaster, particularly in the desert. Another idea was an attachment which could be put into the feedway and which allowed a metal 300-round

feed, for this is unique among machine guns. The gun used a flat tin tray holding 20 rounds in clips, very like the Hotchkiss feed, though upside down with the rounds on the under side. The bolt pushed each round straight forward out of the clip and into the chamber, but when the empty case was extracted it was ingeniously (and quite unnecessarily) put back into the same clip! When the 20 rounds were fired the tray fell out of the right side of the gun, holding all 20 empty cases. As a means of keeping the battlefield tidy this method has had few equals, but as a practical way of operating a machine gun it seems ridiculous. However, to be charitable, the idea was probably to save a large ejection opening and

belt to be used instead of the box, and with this the rounds were actually greased, so that they picked up the maximum amount of grit. But at least 300 rounds were better than six sets of 50 in boxes.

The water-cooled barrel of 1914 was dropped and an air-cooled one substituted with a provision for changing on much the same lines as with the Model 30 Breda, and this was quite successful, but two other ideas were not. One was a decelerator, put in to cut down the rate of fire and give the fluted chamber a chance to work. It brought the fire down from 500 rpm to 120, which was utterly useless for a support gun. The other was a change to allow the gun to fire from a closed bolt, in order to improve accuracy. Again, this must have been done without any sort of trial at all, since once the barrel got hot it cooked any rounds waiting in the chamber, with the usual dangerous results, and back came that deadly cocking rod which was still left out in the open. All told it is difficult to find anything kind to say about this gun, but it was made in substantial numbers and saw the war through from beginning to end.

The final improvement came from the Breda firm, which in 1937 brought out their medium gun. This was undoubtedly more satisfactory than either of the other two, though by no means beyond criticism. It was a fairly conventional gas-operated gun with an air-cooled barrel for which there was provision for a quick and easy change; the gas regulator had ten settings to compensate for different conditions over a wide range. Unfortunately it inherited the habits of its predecessors in not having a satisfactory primary extraction for the fired case, and once more the case was jerked sharply from the chamber with the inevitable results of torn bases and jams. Once more the only remedy was to grease the ammunition, and once more this led to jams, but this time not so badly. The fascination about the Model 37 lies in its

54

the designer must have argued that as he had to have a slot for the empty tray to come out of, there was no point in adding more holes than he could help.

Despite the peculiarities, the Model 37 was rated as a good gun and it remained in service until 1945, though it must have been less effective than it needed with that restricted feed of only 20 rounds. It is difficult to imagine a gun team putting up a very effective shoot when they had to stop to reload after every burst. However, the gun certainly looks a better job than any of the others then in service in Italy, and in 1938 it was modified to take a vertical box magazine on top of the body, much like a Bren. This model was not for the infantry

– it went into tanks, armoured cars and self-propelled guns. Because barrel-changing is almost impossible in vehicles it was given a much thicker one and a pistol-grip instead of two spade-handles. Why no attempt was made to give it a belt-feed is a complete mystery, but the designers of Italian machine guns were always strange in their ways.

All told the Italian infantry was not well served in its machine guns during World War II. One hopes that the military hierarchy who were responsible for lumbering the battalions with these weapons had to do a spell of duty in the field and see for themselves what they had given the unfortunate units to use.

Breda Modello 1937		
Ammunition	8mm Cartuccia Pallotola Modello 35	
Length	50in	1270mm
Weight unloaded	43lb	19.5kg
Barrel	26.75in	679mm
Magazine	20-round strip	
Cyclic rate	450rpm	
Muzzle velocity	2600ft/sec	791m/sec

Anti-Tank Rifles

Italy never produced a native design for an anti-tank rifle, but relied instead on using foreign purchases or captured stock. Even then she was a little slow in starting. The reasoning is hard to follow, since the lessons of the Spanish Civil War were clearly realized by all who had taken part, and Italy had played as big a part as any nation. But somehow the idea of light portable anti-tank weapons within the platoon was not grasped. In other respects the lesson was well taken, and anti-tank platoons in the infantry regiment had a 47mm towed gun which, for 1936, had a reasonable performance. But there were never enough of these guns to issue them down to individual battalions, except for special tasks, and in 1941 the infantry unit was virtually without its own defence against armoured vehicles.

This lack became quite clear when the first battles were fought in the desert, and in a rush to make up the shortage Italy bought guns from Switzerland. To be fair, she had bought a few before the war started, but after 1941 the need became urgent. She also got a few more from Germany, which did not like the heavy Swiss design, and finally about 2,000 captured Polish Model 1935s were handed over from the loot taken by the German Army. By late 1941 the picture looked a bit better.

The Swiss Solothurn which was purchased was derived from the S.18/100 of about 1932. This was a remarkable gun, being compact, powerful and reasonably light. It came from a Rheinmetall gun of World War I through the fact that Rheinmetall owned Solothurn and used them as a way of getting round the Versailles Treaty. The S.18/100 was sold to a few European countries but was not a great success. For one thing it was too expensive, and for another it was not quite powerful enough despite the fact that it was 20mm calibre and had a muzzle velocity of 1,830ft/sec (600m/sec). So it was redesigned to take a more powerful round and called the S.18/1000. This was a far better proposition and could take on light tanks at 500m without difficulty. What was difficult was moving the thing – it was 7ft 1in long (2.17m) and weighed 120lb (54.5kg) and it was nearly always found with a light two-wheeled mount which was either dragged by the crew or towed with a light vehicle. It was beautifully made, and most expensive to buy. It was a self-loader, feeding from a hefty magazine on the left side which carried ten rounds. There was a version which fired full automatic, but this was pretty hopeless from the gunner's point of view since he could never hold it on the target after the first shot and the rest of the magazine simply spread itself around the target area. So bad was the recoil that there was a most elaborate muzzle-brake, carefully designed to balance the reduction of recoil against the shattering noise that it made at the crew positions.

Oddly enough, the earlier S.18/100, which had fired a less powerful cartridge, had much better arrangements for absorbing recoil, but it could only be fired on full automatic

so perhaps it needed them. Anyway, loading the 1000 was quite a trick. The cocking handle was a crank on the right of the body and it had to be turned three and a half times to pull the breech block to the rear, which it did by winding a length of bicycle chain around a sprocket. The handle was then turned back again for the requisite three and a half turns and a full magazine slapped into the housing on the left side, whereupon, with a great noise of moving machinery, the 10lb (4.5kg) breech block slammed forward and chambered a 20mm round. From then on it was just a matter of pulling the trigger and hanging on hard to the pistol grip and butt, trying not to wince at each shot. The extreme range was over 1,500m, but the best battle range for taking on armour was about 500, and it was recommended that the gunner aimed for the sides and back of the vehicle as even a 20mm solid shot was too light for the front of light tanks in 1940.

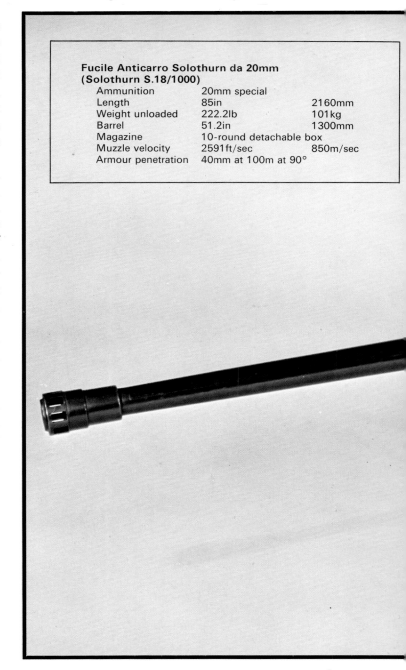

Fucile Anticarro Solothurn da 20mm (Solothurn S.18/1000)

Ammunition	20mm special	
Length	85in	2160mm
Weight unloaded	222.2lb	101kg
Barrel	51.2in	1300mm
Magazine	10-round detachable box	
Muzzle velocity	2591ft/sec	850m/sec
Armour penetration	40mm at 100m at 90°	

These very good guns were issued on a scale of two or three per battalion, though there were never enough to go round when they were needed, and one of their troubles was that they required at least three men in the crew. They were therefore anything but a platoon weapon, and this was what was wanted for the infantry. The shortage was made up with captured stocks of Polish M.35 rifles. In 1935 the Polish Army had accepted this one-man anti-tank rifle, which had been designed under the leadership of Jaroslav Mareszek and which at the time was probably the best among the very few existing in the world.

The M.35 was little more than a modernized 1918 Mauser with a five-shot magazine, and it fired the same 7.92mm bullet with a tungsten core. The cartridge case was lengthened to take more propellant and the bullet had a velocity of 4,200ft/sec (1,275m/sec) at the muzzle. This gave it enough penetration for the light armoured vehicles of that day, and the Poles were so pleased with their rifle that they put it into production in Warsaw under the strictest secrecy. Unfortunately they seem to have let security run away with itself because they issued very few, and these were kept under severe restrictions. By the time of the German invasion in 1939 there were between one and two thousand in the stores, but virtually none of the units had them, nor were they trained to use them.

The needs of their Italian allies became so pressing that the Germans handed over the entire stock of captured Polish rifles, and the Italian Army produced its own operating manual and put the gun into service as quickly as possible. As a stopgap it had its uses, but by 1940 it was already out of date and by 1942, by when very few were left in use, it had become an embarrassment. Hardly any survived the war.

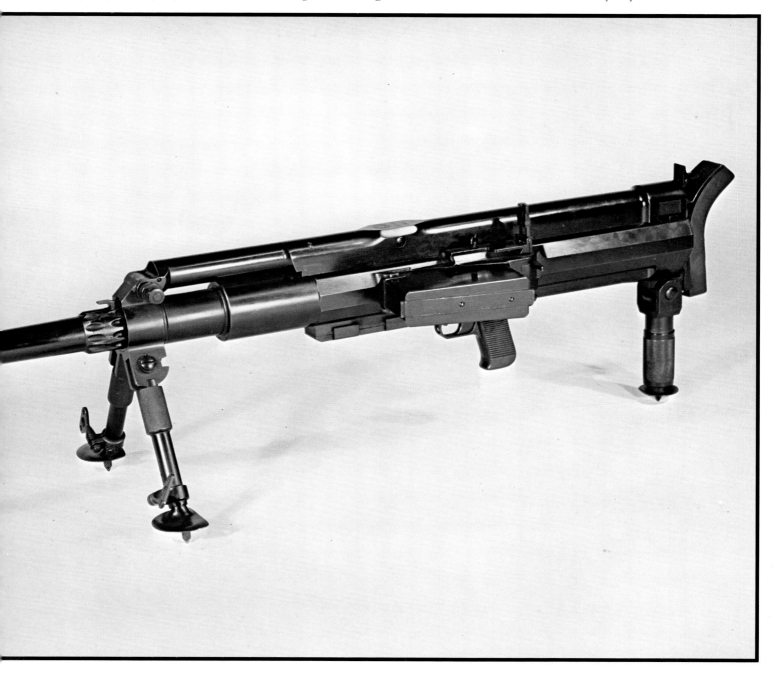

JAPAN

There are several features which make Japanese small arms unique in World War II, and none are in themselves very prominent. It is the mixture of them which marks the national weapons in a peculiar and distinctive way. There is something about the look of the Japanese weapons of this era which makes them immediately recognizable among those of other nations. Mostly this is an ungainly or un-balanced outline; for a nation whose artistic talents are so great the appearance of some of its infantry weapons comes as a surprise. The Arisaka rifle is on its own ordinary enough, but put the Japanese bayonet on the muzzle and it is immediately out of proportion. Similarly with the machine guns, which for the most part are characterized by strangely shaped butts apparently flimsily attached to the body. The Model 97 anti-tank rifle is a mass of bits and pieces sticking out at all angles. They all look awkward, and one wonders whether any of these weapons were ever designed as a whole or just put together from a set of parts.

In fact, design does seem to have been one of the chief difficulties in the early years of the century, when the basis of the small-arms family was being laid down. The Arisaka was a Mauser adapted by a committee, and despite this handicap it was a remarkably successful weapon. Other weapons however, were not so lucky. Most of them fell under the control of Lieutenant General (as he finally became) Kijiro Nambu. He studied weapons from an early age, and became the Japanese Army chief adviser and designer in 1910. From then on practically every weapon that came into military service bore his influence, and it is unfortunate that that influence was often not for the best. He set up his own rifle works in 1927, retired in 1937 and remained as a con-sultant until 1943. His reputation among the Japanese hierarchy seems to have been formidable, although for the most part he confined himself to modifying existing foreign designs and produced very little that was original.

The other aspect of Japanese small arms that is most difficult to unravel without a careful study is the ammunition. The types and sub-types are a perpetual trap to the unwary, and it will be as well as to outline the main versions so that the reader can refer back to it while going through this section.

Firstly, the pistol ammunition was the 8mm Nambu, which did not change.

Next was the 6.5mm Arisaka round, a semi-rimmed straightforward round dating from 1905, known as the Model 38 (the Japanese dating system is explained later). Unfortunately this round was too powerful for the light machine guns, and so there was a Model 38 (1905) 6.5mm reduced-power round, which could only be recognized by looking at the packs. In 1931 in the campaign in Manchuria it became apparent that this 6.5mm ammunition was not up to modern standards, and a 7.7mm (.303in) round was intro-duced for the Model 92 (1932) version of the Hotchkiss

medium machine gun. This was again semi-rimmed, but in 1939 it was also made as rimless, and this fitted the Model 99 (1939) rifle and machine gun. Finally there was the 7.7mm rimmed round, which was none other than the original British .303in copied without alteration. No attempt ever seems to have been made by the Japanese to specify which was which, so that the quotation of calibre of a weapon does no more than narrow the field in which it lies. It does not identify it. Nambu must have been responsible for much of this extraordinary confusion, since it started during his time of greatest influence.

One can imagine that the life of a Japanese ammunition ordnance officer must have been a continual nightmare, for all this ammunition was in service at the same time – it must not be thought that one followed the other; each was brought into service alongside the others. So at any one time there were at least five different types of rifle-calibre ammunition, in two distinct calibres. Actually there were a few more besides, made for special weapons, but these can be ignored.

A further difficulty in the Japanese small-arms world was the shortage of factory capacity. By coming late into the modern industrial field Japan had no spare capacity remaining from earlier years. All industrial expansion had been planned for specific reasons, and heavy industry for ship-building and railways had taken priority at first. The sort of light engineering industry that builds small arms in quantity was not easily available, and its standards were fairly low. Much of Nambu's early efforts were directed towards altering the Hotchkiss designs down to a level that his native firms could make with success. This is one reason for the low-powered 6.5mm round of 1905, for it put less strain on the weapons and allowed them to be made to lower specifications of strength and accuracy. When Japan was building up her armaments in the 1930s there was even less factory space.

Finally, one cannot start a study of Japanese weapons, however brief, without a short explanation of the workings of the Japanese calendar. Before the death of the Emperor Meiji in 1912 all ordnance was designated by the year of his reign; thus the Model 38 Arisaka rifle was introduced in 1905 and the Model 44 in 1911. Meiji died in 1912 and Emperor Taisho reigned until 1925, so the numbering changed and 1914 became year 3, while 1922 produced the Model 11 light machine gun. If that seems logical, worse is to follow. Emperor Hirohito came to the throne in 1925, and so once again the numbering changed, but not for all – for after Taisho it was decided that the numbering should run from one fixed base-line, and the year of the start of the Japanese Empire was selected. This made 1929 into 2589 and 1941 into 2601, though it was also known as Showa 16, from the Hirohito sequence which had not been entirely replaced. Worse still, the Empire system of numbering was often reduced to one digit; thus 1940 was 2600 and became 0 for some weapons, but it could also be 100! Thus, the famous Zero fighter plane was introduced in 1940, but so was the Model 100 submachine gun.

14 Nen Shiku Kenju (Type 04 Nambu)		
Ammunition	8mm Taisho 14	
Length	8.93in	227mm
Weight unloaded	2lb	.90kg
Barrel	4.75in	121mm
Magazine	8-round detachable box	
Muzzle velocity	1050ft/sec	320m/sec

As with so many other weapons, Japanese pistols were undistinguished in design and also in performance. There were fewer different types than there were among other weapons, and fairly small production numbers. As a general rule only officers carried pistols; there does not seem to have been the more general issue to such soldiers as despatch riders and military police which was the case in the Allied armies.

The pistols themselves were largely handicapped by the ammunition they fired. The Japanese plumped for automatic pistols rather than revolvers before World War I and designed their own pistol round, a relatively weak 8mm which had no counterpart elsewhere in the world. On the whole this does not seem to have been any trouble to the Japanese, who only used pistols infrequently and so were presumably never embarrassed by shortages of ammunition in the field. The oldest pistol, which was the model 04, came into service in 1915. It is more generally known as the Nambu, after its designer, though this name was later applied to the next model. The 04 generally resembled the Luger Parabellum in outline shape, though its action was anything but similar.

This first Nambu probably owed more to the Italian Glisenti for its inspiration than any other, and it suffered from a few defects which the original did not. Among these was a weak mechanism, some deficiencies in safety, and a tendency for the striker spring to weaken quickly and fail to fire the cartridges. As with so many pistols of its day it was provided with a highly optimistic leaf backsight graduated up to 500m, but had an eight-round magazine in the butt. It was susceptible to dust and dirt, and it was not reliable in action.

In 1925 Nambu modernized the pistol, eradicating most of the early drawbacks and making some improvements, not least to the production processes required to make it. Sadly, there were still some odd features. One was the safety, which could only be operated by the firer's left hand as it was on the right side of the slide. Another was the holding-open device which came into play when the magazine was empty; this

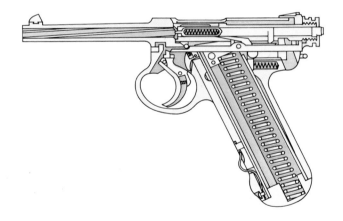

worked by the bolt actually catching on the magazine platform, thereby fairly effectively jamming it in place. The empty magazine could only be grasped by two small wooden knobs at its base, and a combination of cold and wet fingers usually failed completely to remove it. There is a record of a Japanese officer in Burma who was shot while wrestling with a magazine which his sweating hand could not pull out.

This pistol was modified in the early 1930s in substantial numbers to accept a gloved finger for winter fighting in Manchuria. The larger guard looks rather odd, and is unmistakable once noted. Apparently no other Japanese pistol was so changed. A variant of the Nambu was the 'Baby Nambu', a 7mm version of the original 04 model, though it did not appear until the 1930s. This pistol was

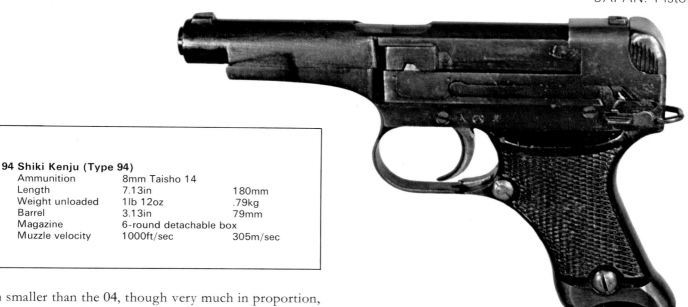

94 Shiki Kenju (Type 94)

Ammunition	8mm Taisho 14	
Length	7.13in	180mm
Weight unloaded	1lb 12oz	.79kg
Barrel	3.13in	79mm
Magazine	6-round detachable box	
Muzzle velocity	1000ft/sec	305m/sec

much smaller than the 04, though very much in proportion, and was intended for commercial sale. However, it seems that none reached the market. All were taken over by the Japanese Air Force, though there is now doubt as to whether more than 3,000 were made.

Both of the Nambu pistols were quite difficult to manufacture, and in an attempt to find a more suitable pistol for mass production the Type 94 was introduced. This appeared in 1934 and on first sight appeared to be a fairly normal automatic pistol, though with an oddly curved butt. In fact it was a thoroughly bad pistol and a potential danger to its user and his companions. Why the Japanese chose to design this strange weapon when there were so many proven types which they could have copied is still a mystery; perhaps it was misguided nationalism. The Type 94 has little to recommend it, and much to condemn it.

It was a recoil-operated pistol, locked by a vertical sliding block cammed into place. This was quite strong enough for the 8mm cartridge, though it would not do for anything more powerful. The short barrel dropped the muzzle velocity and hence the muzzle energy to a lower level than almost any other military pistol that has ever been accepted for service, making it comparatively ineffective at more than quite close range.

A mechanical safety in the trigger mechanism ensured that the hammer could not be operated until the action was locked, but this feature soon wore and allowed the round to be fired from an open breech. This was not as dangerous as might be supposed, due to the feeble cartridge. Another danger lay in the poor linkage from trigger to hammer. This ran along the outside of the slide on the left side, and when the hammer was cocked it could be released by squeezing this link, or by dropping the pistol, left side downwards. A further little misery was that the magazine was jammed by the bolt when empty, as in the Nambu types. All told, it was an unfortunate choice of a weapon. Although many thousands were made, they must have been unpopular, since almost none turned up in action. It is thought that the main users were the Japanese Air Force.

Hand-Operated Rifles

The Japanese Army fought throughout the Second World War with the same, or nearly the same, bolt-action rifles as it used in the First World War, and these both derived from the 1905 model Arisaka. The Arisaka was named after a colonel of that name who headed a panel of technical experts which produced the rifle, itself a straight adaptation of the Mauser and no great improvement on it either. The calibre was 6.5mm, and by 1940 this was well out of date. It was a low-power round which lacked penetration and accuracy; this was recognized in Japan in the early 1930s when the deficiencies had shown up clearly in the fighting in Manchuria. As a result the 7.7mm round was introduced to replace it, but the 6.5mm remained in service throughout the war.

The Arisaka which bore the brunt of the Pacific fighting was the type Meiji 38 (or Model 1905, since the 38th year of the reign of the Emperor Meiji was in that year). This was a perfectly undistinguished carbine version of the rifle with a five-round internal magazine, a typically clumsy early Mauser bolt-action, and a cleaning rod projecting under the muzzle. It is so similar to the German Mauser 98K that one has to look twice to tell them apart. The greatest difference lay in the bayonet, a great wicked thing nearly half as long as the carbine itself. There was also the long rifle version, and both seem to have been used without much attempt at rationalization.

When the 7.7mm round was brought in the old Meiji 38 was up-dated to fire it and then became the Model 99 (1939). The only real differences were in the calibre and the chamber, barrel and face of the bolt, so that clear identification is difficult until one actually handles the weapon. It had no more to recommend it than its predecessors, though it was relatively cheap to make, reliable and strong. Most of the

Arisaka Model 1905 (Meiji 38th Year Type)

Ammunition	6.5mm Meiji 30	
Length	50.25in	1275mm
Weight unloaded	9lb 8oz	4.31kg
Barrel	31.45in	789mm
Magazine	5-round integral box	
Muzzle velocity	2400ft/sec	730m/sec

Type 99 rifles carried a light wire monopod under the fore-end of the stock, and this rather flimsy contraption was intended to steady the weapon for firing. Despite several attempts with more than one rifle, the author has never yet managed to get a comfortable firing position with one of these monopods, and it remains a mystery how the small Japanese soldier ever used it. However, the general idea is quite good and appears today on many modern self-loading rifles, though in a more practical form.

There were several different variants of the Type 99. The most usual ones are those already described, either a long rifle or a shorter carbine, but there was also a paratroop version of the rifle. This was prepared for parachuting in a rather different way from other Japanese weapons, because its barrel unscrewed at the breech, or rather it came apart at the breech, since the connection was not quite as secure as could have been achieved with a simple screw. It was held with a type of bayonet catch, locked with a pin and lug, but

Far right: Japanese troops taking part in the Manchurian campaign which was a proving-ground for infantry weapons. A variety of small arms can be seen in this picture, but Arisaka 1905 rifles and the Type 11 machine gun (lower right) predominate. The Arisaka rifle was basically a straight adaptation of the Mauser and no improvement upon it.

both tended to come apart after quite a modest number of rounds had been fired. A modification was therefore introduced in which the actual barrel connection was simpler, but the lock arrangements were stronger. This appears to have been successful, but at the best of times these folding rifles were never meant to have a long life. Others were given a folding hinge at the small of the butt – a shocking way to do it, since this is the weakest part of the stock, and the part subjected to most stress in normal carriage and general banging around in the soldier's hands. As a result the hinge had to be strong and heavy, and was not at all pleasant to handle.

The Japanese were given a formidable reputation for sniping by the Allies, and the newspapers of 1941 and 1942 carry numbers of stories of snipers hiding in trees and picking off the troops walking below. Just to colour the story more these snipers were always tied to the trees so that they did not fall down when shot, and nobody ever knew whether the bundle in the tree was alive or not. Again there were eye-witness accounts of live Japanese shamming dead and opening up on the rear of a column, and a host of similar bogey stories which gave the Japanese infantryman a reputation for skilful killing and cunning which he scarcely deserved. The so-called snipers were really sharpshooters, the difference being that they were frequently not good shots at all, but the short ranges of jungle warfare meant that they could scarcely miss. Far from being selective in their targets, as good snipers should be, they tended to shoot anyone who came near. However, many of them did use a special sniping version of the Type 97 (1937) 6.5mm rifle. This sniping rifle was the normal 6.5mm fitted with a low-power telescopic sight on the left of the receiver, and with the bolt handle bent over so that the hand cleared the underside of the scope when reloading. Some were fitted with the Type 99 wire monopod. The great advantage of the 6.5mm round was that it was comparatively quiet and so not easy to locate in jungle; at short ranges its lack of power was not significant.

The Arisakas were perfectly adequate weapons, though elderly, and they were made in enormous quantities up to, and during, the war. There are now no surviving records of the exact numbers produced, but it is popularly supposed that there must have been over 10,000,000 in all, covering the whole lifetime of the design. The ones built after 1943 are clearly recognizable because the finish and standard are poor and such items as the sights are crude and inefficient. The metal tends to be below specification so that moving parts wear quickly, and in some of the last versions the workmanship is so bad that the levels of safety must have been affected.

Strangely the Japanese never opted for a self-loading rifle, nor even appear to have bought any foreign models for trials. There were some abortive tests with home-produced types in 1922 but nothing came of them, and the idea seems to have been discarded except for a tiny number of copies of the Garand. These may have been prototypes for a production run, or may simply have been used for general research.

Submachine Guns

With their policy of overseas domination and dedication to mass infantry tactics, one would expect the Japanese Army to have taken to the submachine gun in large numbers, for it is ideally suited to what they had in mind for the Pacific campaigns and the Chinese mainland operations. In fact, there was surprisingly little interest shown in submachine guns until 1935 or so, though the Japanese Navy bought and tested a few German Bergmanns in the early 1930s and there was apparently some talk of licensing manufacture. It never came to anything, and the few specimens that were bought are unlikely to have seen action.

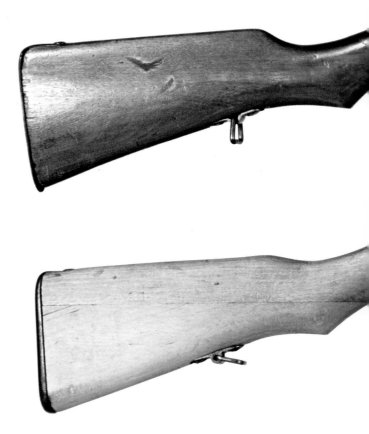

In 1935 a new Japanese design appeared known as the Model 1. This was fairly uninspired and rather heavy. It had some outline connections with the early Finnish Suomi designs, but it seems to have lacked the Suomi robustness and freedom from trouble, for it was not a success and was soon dropped. It fired the weak and not very effective 8mm pistol round, which may have been part of its failing. Anyway, in 1937 the Model 2 appeared, which was if anything rather worse. It fired a special 6.5mm round, which had no counterpart anywhere else and was in any case too weak. There was now some fairly furious back-stage work in the design departments and in 1940 the Model 3 was unveiled. With the Pacific war quite obviously just round the corner, and a substantial one already raging in China, the Model 3 was accepted and put into production as the Type 100.

It is possible to see several strains in the ancestry of the Type 100. At first glance it seems to owe something to Beretta, Suomi and Bergmann, and no doubt it did. Unfortunately, in the combination the desirable features of these guns got lost, and the only prominent ones that were left were the ones that the designer might well have chosen to do without. Reliability was poor; the round was once more the feeble 8mm; the weight was high and the length considerable. Nevertheless, it was a workable design. Rather too much trouble was taken to make sure that a bayonet could be fixed

100 Shiki Kikantanju (Type 100)		
Ammunition	8mm Taisho 14	
Length	35in	889mm
Weight unloaded	8lb 8oz	3.83kg
Barrel	9in	228mm
Magazine	30-round detachable box	
Cyclic rate	450rpm	
Muzzle velocity	1100ft/sec	335m/sec

100 Shiki Kikantanju (Type 100, 1944 pattern)		
Ammunition	8mm Taisho14	
Length	36in	863mm
Weight unloaded	8lb 8oz	3.83kg
Barrel	9in	228mm
Magazine	30-round detachable box	
Cyclic rate	800rpm	
Muzzle velocity	1100ft/sec	335m/sec

to the barrel, which seems to indicate that somebody had his priorities wrong. There was a complicated sliding-ramp backsight and even a bipod on a few versions, making one wonder if the military had quite grasped what a submachine gun is meant to do. In its favour was the fact that the interior of the barrel was chrome-plated, a feature which gave it a long life and a tremendous resistance to dirt. It only fired automatic, though at the slow rate of 450 rounds per minute, which is slow enough to allow the firer to control the rise of the muzzle and keep the group to a reasonable size.

The magazine was the usual box, feeding in from the left-hand side, but to accommodate the rimmed 8mm round it had to be curved, and it was liable to jam unless clean.

Parachutists had a folding-butt version, in the Japanese tradition, with the hinge at the small of the butt. How many were made is not at all clear now, but it was undoubtedly few by the standards of Western nations. As the design was not too successful, the production seems to have been kept low to allow time for it to be finalized – or it may be that the

factories just could not cope anyway. However, throughout the war the Type 100 was slowly and progressively improved, resulting in the final version in 1944 in which the recoil spring was changed to increase the rate of fire to 800 rpm and the bayonet bar was removed. A bayonet could still be fixed on the muzzle, and the muzzle also had a compensator cut into it to reduce the muzzle climb, which it only partially managed to do. The optimistic backsight disappeared and there were other minor changes to make the design easier and cheaper to manufacture, but it was already too late, and probably no more than 7,000 were built and issued. Few if any reached the front-line troops, and most were captured by the occupying US forces in 1945.

Machine Guns

From the very beginning the Japanese recognized that machine guns were useful infantry weapons, and they took the Hotchkiss Model 1897 in 1902 and used it with great success in the Russo-Japanese war of 1905. This convinced them of the wisdom of machine-gun warfare, and from then on they continually experimented with different types. However, all of these types were really just versions of the basic Hotchkiss designs of the late nineteenth century. Behind all the bizarre shapes of the subsequent models with their confusing type-numbers there is the original Hotchkiss gas system and locking arrangements. The pity of it is that the Japanese could not see the sense in leaving well alone. Colonel Nambu of pistol fame set to work to adapt the design to take the 6.5mm cartridge. At the same time he could not resist the temptation to change a few features, with the result that his Type 3 (1914) was rather less good than its parent. The main difference lay in the fact that he slightly altered the breech-opening characteristics in order to allow for the lack of cartridge head-space adjustment. This change resulted in a violent jerk as the cartridge was pulled out, whereas the Hotchkiss had the usual 'primary extraction' movement. Like other guns which used this jerking principle, Nambu found that he had to oil the cases before feeding, and so the Hotchkiss body had to be adapted to take an oil reservoir and meter.

In 1932 the gun was modified to take the 7.7mm semi-rimmed round, and it then became the Type 92. The differences were small, apart from the obvious ones of chamber and barrel. The oiling system remained because there was still no primary extraction, but a flash hider was fitted to the muzzle to cope with the greater output from the new round. Another change was that the two spade grips were hung below the body, looking a little like a couple of pistol grips side by side. The greatest drawback to this rather pedestrian gun was its weight. It weighed 122lb (55.55kg) with its tripod, and there had to be some special arrangements for the small Japanese soldier to lift this load. Each tripod leg had a socket near the bottom, and poles were slipped into the two front ones. In the rear one went a curved steel tube not unlike a pair of handlebars. Three men could now pick up the entire gun and tripod and carry it as one unit without having to take it apart; for short hauls over reasonable ground it was an ideal method, and very fast. In an attempt to reduce the weight the Type 01 (1941) was introduced in 1941, in which the total was down to 81lb (39kg) and there were a few other changes too. The machining was simplified, but few of these guns were actually made and they never appeared in quantity.

The Type 92 (1932) was quite robust and reliable and became an excellent weapon for giving supporting fire. It fired slowly at 450 rpm, and the Allies gave it the nickname 'Woodpecker', but it was most effective when suitably sited. Although all production stopped in 1945, many of the guns continued in use among the smaller armies of the Far East until well on into the 1950s.

For a light machine gun the Japanese had the Type 11 (1922), another of Nambu's creations. As with so many of the Japanese weapons, this one looked ugly and wrongly balanced. There were two long bipod legs set at the muzzle, a heavily finned barrel, and a square butt looking as if it had been tacked on afterwards and resembling nothing more than a flag, waving from under the body. The small of the butt had a very thin section and had to be made of steel to give it the necessary strength; it was attached to a large

square of wood, offset to the right so as to bring the sights in front of the firer's face. The sights were offset to the right side of the gun because, so it was said, the Japanese cannot close one eye like Europeans can, and so the sights had to allow both eyes to be open. This is nonsense, of course, but the story has held sway for many years now.

The other oddity of the Type 11 (1922) was the feed, unique among machine guns. The gun was intended from the start to be the main firepower of the infantry section (squad), and so Nambu arranged that it could be fed with rifle clips. There was a hopper on the left side which took six five-round clips, laid on their sides and held in place by a spring cover. The feeding claws stripped rounds out of the lower clip and pushed them to the right into the gun, dropping the empty clip out through the bottom. The gunner could see exactly how much ammunition he had left in the hopper, and could top up with clips at any time. Theoretically ideal, the result was less satisfactory. For one thing the

Below: Japanese naval cadets train with a Taisho 3 machine gun. Like the French Hotchkiss from which it was derived, this gun used a flat strip for loading.

modified Hotchkiss mechanism still needed oiled cases, so there was the same reservoir and oiling brush as on the Type 3 (1914), and the same ability to attract dust and dirt into the interior. Worse than this was the fact that Nambu's modifications had meant that the gun fired too quickly with the standard 6.5mm round, and the feed mechanism could not stand up to the battering it got. A special reduced-power round had to be provided, loaded with 2 grams of propellant instead of 2.15 grams, and the whole concept of the complicated hopper-feed was lost.

The restrictions of the Type 11 (1922) were recognized soon enough, but it was the mid-1930s before anything was done about it and the Type 96 (1936) was introduced. This was a light gun with traces of descent from the Czech ZB series. It had the same fully finned barrel, flat-sided body, drum backsight, underslung gas cylinder, carrying handle

and top-feed magazine. But there the similarity ended, because the action was still basically the same as in the Type 11 (1922), and so was the round. Incredibly, it was still necessary to use the reduced-power round and each round had to be oiled, but the method changed. There was no reservoir on the gun; the ammunition was oiled as it was loaded into the magazine. This meant that the gun team carried oily ammunition with them, and any magazine dropped into the dirt carried grinding paste into the breech. The number and complexity of stoppages was phenomenal, but under ideal conditions it was at least as good a gun as any European one of its time. It had two peculiarities: one was the ability to fix a bayonet beneath the muzzle, a need which arose from the Japanese requirement to carry the gun at the hip during the assault; the other was a low-powered telescopic sight. The telescope is all but unique for a machine gun. It gave a 2.5 magnification and fitted into a small dovetail on the right rear of the body. The scope itself was offset to the right, leaving the iron sights clear on the left side.

The Type 99 (1939) was the logical development of the Type 96 and came into service in 1939 when it was realized from the conflict with China that the 6.5mm round was too weak for modern war. The new 7.7mm ammunition demanded rather more changes than just re-barrelling and re-chambering. The manufacturing tolerances had to be closer, and for some parts different materials were needed. The

changes were more than Japanese industry could easily accommodate, and few of these guns were actually issued to the army until 1942. By 1943 it was actually in battle, and from then on the production rose steadily until at the end of the war it was becoming the dominant combat machine gun on land. Probably its greatest advantage over the Type 96 was that, due to better machining of the breech and its fitting, the cartridge head space could be adjusted. This did away with the need to oil the cartridges. A gas regulator with five different holes allowed for ideal balancing of the gas system, and the result was a reliable and effective gun, albeit expensive to make due to the amount of machining required.

By intelligent and aggressive use of these light machine guns the Japanese were able to extract the most from them, and at the same time to give themselves a reputation for good shooting (which they probably did not deserve) and concealment (which they undoubtedly did deserve). They were not beyond using light machine guns as sniping weapons, nor of mounting an ambush with only one light machine gun to provide the firepower. At all times the section light machine gun was carried well forward in the battle and provided the major firepower of the platoon.

A Japanese infantry battalion had 36 light and 8 medium machine guns. The medium versions were grouped together in the machine-gun company in two platoons each of four guns. Each platoon had two sections of two guns and an

Nen Shiki Kikanju 1922 (Type 11)

Ammunition	6.5mm Meiji reduced load	
Length	43.5in	1104mm
Weight unloaded	22lb 8oz	10.19kg
Barrel	19in	482mm
Magazine	30-round hopper	
Cyclic rate	500rpm	
Muzzle velocity	2300ft/sec	701m/sec

Shiki Kikanju 1939 (Type 99)

Ammunition	7.7mm Shiki 99	
Length	46.5in	1104mm
Weight unloaded	23lb	10.43kg
Barrel	21.5in	545mm
Magazine	30-round detachable box	
Cyclic rate	500 rpm	
Muzzle velocity	2350ft/sec	715m/sec

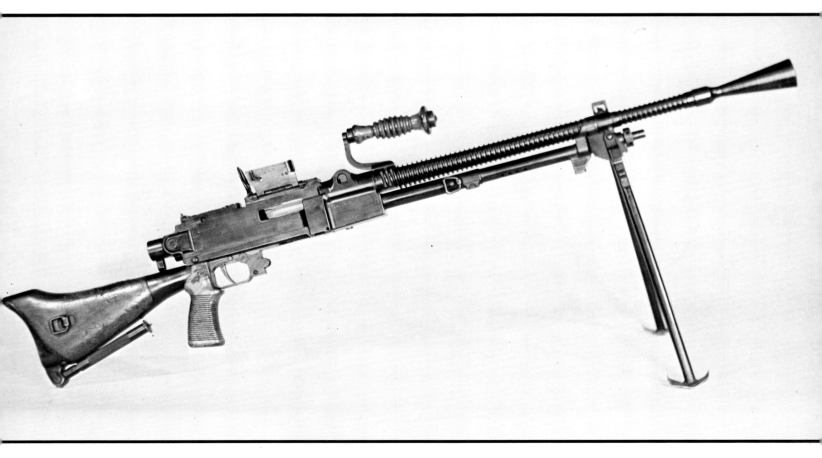

ammunition section. It was the Japanese custom to site single guns, whereas the British and to a lesser extent the US always sited guns in pairs so that they had mutual support. The light machine guns were carried one to each infantry section. There were three sections to a platoon, three platoons to a company, and four companies in the battalion. Strangely, neither company nor battalion headquarters seem to have been allocated any light machine guns for local defence, but these sub-units were always kept very small and presumably relied on the companies for protection. Each light machine gun was serviced by a team of two men, the gunner who carried the gun, and his loader who carried magazines, spotted for fall of shot and provided immediate local protection for the gun position with his rifle and grenades.

There are plenty of examples of the successful use of these machine guns. The British first met the Type 96 in Hong Kong when the Japanese 38th Division attacked the mainland defences in December 1941. From then on it appeared in steadily increasing numbers until 1943, when the Type 99 started to supplant it. The Type 99 (1939) was first met in the Aleutians, as were several other weapons, an indication that the islands were of some importance to the Japanese war plans; but the Type 92 (1932) medium machine gun was universal to all battle areas. It was particularly troublesome on Attu Island in the Aleutians, where the guns were sited with great skill and opened up on the attacking US troops at 1,000m or more. At other times they were used for harassing fire at ranges of over 2,000m, when the bullets fell almost vertically and normal foxholes or trenches gave no protection. This steep trajectory at long range made it possible for the gunners to search ground behind hills and folds in the ground and also on the beaches.

The defeat of Japan led to the disappearance of the exact records of the manufacture of weapons during the war and all figures are now guess-work, but it is certain that the Types 92 and 01 must have totalled 20,000 or 30,000 by 1945. For the

Type 96 the number must be at least 120,000 and for the Type 99 it is calculated at just below 100,000.

While the foregoing machine guns were the ones which were the accepted standard issue and the ones most generally found in battle, there were many more in the inventory. Prominent among these were two straight copies of the Vickers medium machine gun and the Lewis light machine gun. Both were used on the ground and in the air, and both were in 7.7mm (.303in) rimmed calibre. The Lewis was made in quite large numbers and was used by the Japanese Navy also. Another gun was the Type 97 (1937), which was a copy of the Czech ZB 26, yet usually used as a tank machine gun. It is difficult to imagine a less suitable weapon for a tank, since it fed from a top magazine, and it is hardly surprising

that it later appeared in use as an infantry gun, fitted with spindly bipod legs and a solid short butt. One feature it retained from its tank use was a long telescopic sight along the left side of the body, and just to complicate the ammunition picture a little further, it fired the 7.7mm rimless round used by the Type 99.

Anti-Tank Rifles

It is a misnomer to talk of Japanese anti-tank rifles in the plural, as there was only one ever in service use. There were rumours of others, in particular a 13mm rifle, and on the Japanese mainland the occupying US forces found several makeshift large-calibre small arms intended apparently to engage landing craft as they approached the beaches. But for the infantry battalions the only anti-tank rifle was the Model 97 (1937) 20mm automatic.

The Model 97 was an original design, though it appears to have similarities with the Hispano-Suiza aircraft cannon, particularly in its use of the combined gas and blowback system of operation. The breech was locked at the moment of firing by the breech-block tipping up at the rear and engaging in lugs in the body. After firing, a gas system unlocked the action, and the remaining pressure in the barrel forced the mechanism to the rear. For 20mm weapons this arrangement was not new at all, but it was efficient – provided that the ammunition did not change during the life of the gun. If it did the gun had to be redesigned to take the new pressures.

As an anti-tank rifle the Model 97 was large, heavy and complicated. It was just over 82in long (2.08m) and weighed 150lb (68kg) complete with its carrying handles. Originally a two-man team was assigned to each gun, but in fact the team was always three and sometimes four. Each battalion had two guns on its establishment, held in an anti-tank platoon in the machine-gun company. Two seems a remarkably small number – most other armies tried to give one

Kyunana Shiki 20mm (Model 97)		
Ammunition	20mm (short case) AT	
Length	80in	2035mm
Weight unloaded	152lb	68.93kg
Barrel	47in	1195mm
Magazine	7-round detachable box	
Muzzle velocity	2000ft/sec	609m/sec

rifle to each infantry platoon – but this is probably because there were never many Model 97s made.

The calibre of 20mm was obviously chosen wisely, since the smaller-bore rifles were outclassed soon after they were designed. It was also sensible since it was in line with other weapons in the Japanese inventory and the same shell could be used as in other cannon, though the cartridge case was special to the 97. The oddity of the Model 97 was that it could only fire at full automatic; there was no provision for single-shot at all. Since the average Japanese soldier was slightly built there had to be elaborate arrangements to absorb the recoil. This was done by making the barrel, body and pistol-grip recoil along a slide. The slide carried the bipod at the front and the butt at the back, with recoil springs and buffers in between, and was so balanced that the recoiling parts never actually got to either extremity of their travel. The firer was thus subjected to one long fluctuating pressure on his shoulder rather than a series of distinct recoil blows. Since the magazine only held seven rounds, no burst of fire could last for long, and apparently a trained gunner was not meant to fire more than two or three at a time anyway. As a further help he had a rear monopod leg under the butt which took the weight at that end and also absorbed some of the backwards push. The snag was that it had to be picked up and shifted if the sight line needed to be traversed, so to shoot at a crossing tank was difficult.

The gunner was usually protected by a thin steel shield which must have offered a theoretical rather than a practical defence, and there was the usual muzzle-brake that every anti-tank rifle had. But the unusual arrangement of the Model 97 was the carriage. As with all Japanese infantry weapons, man-carriage was an essential part of the requirement, and 150lb was well beyond the normal ability of two men with their personal gear as well. So there were special carrying handles. These resembled oversized bicycle handle-bars, and a set was slotted into the front and rear of the recoil slide. One man could take the rear set (or two men could take one handle each) and two men took a handle each at the front. Thus, three or four men could lift and carry the gun quickly and easily without having to touch the hot barrel, or trying to get a grip on folding bipod legs, or catching their clothes in sight brackets, or any of the hundred and one other infuriations which come when one carries a large and heavy weapon in a hurry. The gun could be perfectly safely carried with a loaded magazine, since none of the carrying team had to step in front of the muzzle, and on arriving at the destination the gun could be dropped down pretty well in line for its next task and start firing with scarcely any delay. Some Japanese ideas were not so silly.

Very few of these guns survived the war, lending credence to the theory that not many were made, and there now seem to be no examples of ammunition left at all. One man who fired a captured 97 during the last stages of the Pacific war says that it was remarkably smooth and straightforward, with no more recoil than from a Springfield .30 rifle, and we have to be content with that evaluation.

GREAT BRITAIN

Although British small arms in World War II were not particularly distinguished in either design or general principles, they had the advantage of being backed up by a national policy and plan which was maintained without significant alteration throughout, though that policy can be criticized for being conservative and undistinguished itself. The weapons which had won the First World War were simple, robust, and highly effective in the hands of trained soldiers. With a regular army and no thought of conscripts, the British policy was to continue with these weapons, accepting that to get the best out of them depended more on the user than on the weapon itself, and the only major requirement for the infantry was a suitable light machine gun to replace the complicated and heavy Lewis gun. The financial retrenchment of the 1920s encouraged this attitude and so slow progress was made in modernizing the small-arms inventory.

Some low-key development went into the design of the elderly Lee-Enfield rifle to make it easier to produce in wartime, and a similar exercise was carried out on the pistol, but apart from these minor activities little else was put in hand. The decision was firmly made to stay with the .303in round, which with hindsight was probably wrong from the operational point of view, even though it may have had overwhelming financial pressure which won the day. The rimmed .303 was not a good cartridge to use in machine guns, and most of the European nations had gone away from rims before World War II started. But the British stocks were too large to permit any change, and there was also the Empire to consider, for each of the dominions and colonies used British equipment, and in India there were substantial factories all fully tooled to make .303 weapons and ammunition. So the financiers won the day, as they nearly always do.

The pity of this decision was that as early as 1910 the Small Arms Committee had recommended a change to a smaller rimless calibre than .303, and this had been endorsed by another study in 1922, so there was no lack of argument to support a change. However, whatever the shortcomings of .303 ammunition, it had an excellent ballistic performance, and that saved the day for the army.

The British procurement system was to rely on the government-owned Royal Small Arms Factory for most of the peace-time manufacture and all the peace-time development work, and to go to contracts with industry for wartime expansion and production. This was hardly an encouraging picture for the gun trade, but it worked well enough until 1945. Throughout the lean years after 1918 the firm of BSA (Birmingham Small Arms Ltd) kept their production lines in moth-balls at their own expense against the possibility of another war within the lifetime of the weapons that those lines were capable of making. Their foresight was to prove

horribly correct, and in 1936, when Britain was re-arming as fast as she could, BSA was able to swing into action with the minimum of alterations and delay. Much the same happened at Webley and Scott, another firm with a long and distinguished history in British small arms.

But the greatest manufacturing revolution came with the Sten gun and the bombing of Birmingham. The Sten gun was so simple that it could be made in any little machine shop, and for the first time in Britain military weapons were farmed out to a multitude of tiny firms who could make enormous quantities while remaining more or less immune to bombing. The bombing of the centralized factories in Birmingham accelerated this process of diversion and this all helped to emphasize that while simple designs such as the Sten could be spread around the country, the old solid

weapons could not, and their day was nearly over.

A feature of British small arms for the last hundred years has been the dearth of national designs. Ever since the repeating breech-loaders came into service, the British Army has been equipped with weapons that originated in other countries; perhaps this has been the greatest strength of the British equipment, for there never seems to have been any hesitation in taking whatever is best on the market. This is nowhere more marked than in the selection of the Bren light machine gun, where in many other countries national pride and protection of home industries would probably have forced the choice to go to the home product. In the event this might not have mattered too much, but the Vickers-Berthier only served in India.

The most damaging criticism that can be levelled at the British small-arms policy is that it was appallingly conservative. In fact, one can truthfully say it was almost blind, though so were many other national policies in other countries. Britain failed to appreciate two really major advances that had occurred in, or just after, 1918. The first was the death of the bolt-action rifle, which required far too much skill on the part of the firer to get any sort of reasonable performance from it, and this had been made plain enough by the mass conscript drafts in the latter stages of World War I. Although the Short Lee-Enfield was probably the best bolt-action military rifle that there has been, it was no match for even an average self-loader, and this the British firmly refused to recognize. The next was the value of submachine guns. It took the possibility of defeat from parachutists to ram home the usefulness of this weapon, yet Britain could have had it in quantity long before 1939 and allowed the chance to drop. This is no more short-sighted and incomprehensible than the Japanese, who did the same thing while building up an army to fight in jungle-covered Pacific islands, but that is not an excuse. The fact is that the British looked upon submachine guns as rather unsporting weapons, which is no way to prepare for a war.

Below: British airborne troops at Arnhem, 1944, carrying No. 4 rifles and MK 2 Sten submachine guns.

Pistols have never been a strong point in the British soldier's armoury, and the ones he was given in World War II must be among the least effective and least popular of any. In the first war the standard revolver was the strong, sturdy and entirely reliable old Webley Mark 6, of .455in (11.5mm) calibre. This magnificent hand-gun was the last of a long line of Webleys which had been used in innumerable native wars and skirmishes all over the world, and which had gained the complete faith of their users. Certainly they were heavy – so was their ammunition – but they delivered a knock-down blow with their enormous lead bullet, and they survived indefinite abuse, neglect and damage.

After World War I it was decided that this excellent weapon was too large for normal infantry use, and it required rather too much training to get the best results from it. These criticisms were undoubtedly correct, for the .455 delivers a mighty kick which takes some getting used to, and pistol training is one of those luxuries that never get much attention in wartime. So it was decided to move to a smaller calibre. The Webleys had been built for black-powder ammunition, and had been adapted to the smokeless powders as they appeared, without really changing the essential outlines of the weapon at all. In the 1920s it was possible to get the same stopping power and energy level as the .455 bullet from one that was both smaller and lighter, but which was fired at a higher velocity. The 9mm Parabellum round was a good example at that time of a light but powerful round, and

Webley & Scott Mk VI		
Ammunition	.455in SAA Ball	
Length	11.25in	286mm
Weight unloaded	2lb 6.5oz	1.09kg
Barrel	6in	152mm
Magazine	6-round cylinder	
Muzzle velocity	650ft/sec	199m/sec

it would have been a good thing if the committee which was considering a new pistol had had the sense to adopt it.

Instead they decided to stay with six-shot revolvers, since these were both simple and reliable. Having made that decision they were more or less bound to go to a rimmed cartridge case, and that would not be the 9mm Parabellum. As it turned out it was .38in (9.6mm), and rather less powerful. The revolver chosen was again a Webley, but this time the 1923 Police model, and it was considerably changed in the trigger and lock mechanism by the Royal Small Arms Factory at Enfield. It was then known as the Enfield Revolver, Number 2 and was first issued in 1936.

Although one reason for changing to .38 had been to make a revolver that men could learn to shoot in a short time, the result was not happy. There were men who did very well with it, though one wonders how much ammunition they had to use to get to their standard. But for most of the army,

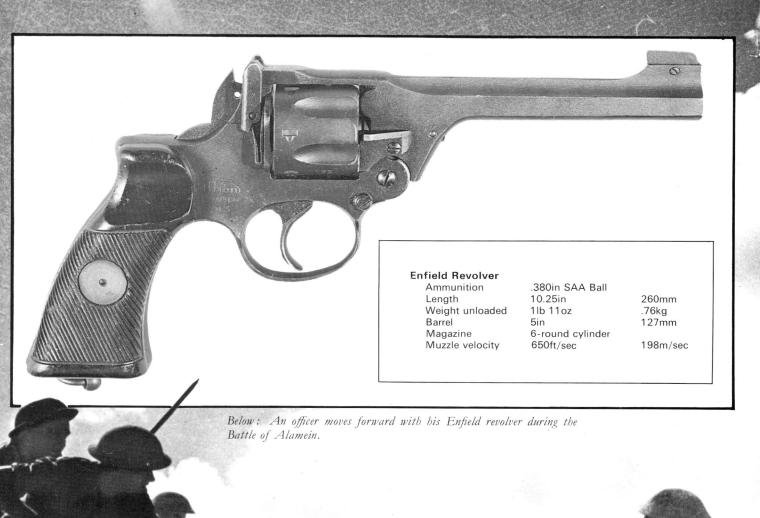

Enfield Revolver

Ammunition	.380in SAA Ball	
Length	10.25in	260mm
Weight unloaded	1lb 11oz	.76kg
Barrel	5in	127mm
Magazine	6-round cylinder	
Muzzle velocity	650ft/sec	198m/sec

Below: An officer moves forward with his Enfield revolver during the Battle of Alamein.

given the ludicrous training allocation of 12 rounds *per year*, there was never much hope of doing better than frightening the opposition by a display of determination. The equipment for carrying the unfortunate weapon did nothing to help either. The issue holster was made of webbing, and a flap buttoned down over the butt so securely that it often took two hands to get it undone. A thick lanyard had to be attached to the butt ring and worn round the neck, where it caught in anything that came near it. Six spare rounds were stowed in webbing loops outside the holster, from which they could only be prised by means of the cleaning rod.

At least this mania for security ensured that nobody actually shot anyone by practising cowboy 'quick draws', but there was not a great deal of confidence in the revolver at the best of times. It was always supposed that the bullet lacked stopping power, which was not true, as it had roughly the same muzzle energy as the old Webley, though rather less momentum due to its lighter weight; but it made men unsure of its effectiveness.

In fact the Enfield was used widely, and made in large quantities. It was issued to all officers as a side-arm, and also to machine gunners, mortar-men, despatch-riders, military police and tank crews. The tank men quickly found that the comb of the hammer caught in their turrets, and a Mark 2 version was produced for them with the comb removed. This revolver could only be double-action, and was even less accurate than the Mark 1, due to the enormous trigger pressure required to operate it. Unfortunately, it was found easier under the stress of war-time manufacturing to change all Enfields to Mark 2, since this simplified the issuing also. The result was that in time the majority of Enfields were double-action, and they then got a very poor reputation.

In contrast to the Enfield was the American Smith & Wesson .38, which was bought in quantity from the USA to

Browning Hi-Power, 9mm SAA Ball		
Ammunition	9mm Parabellum	
Length	7.75in	197mm
Weight unloaded	2lb 3oz	.99kg
Barrel	4.65in	118mm
Magazine	13-round detachable box	
Muzzle velocity	1110ft/sec	335m/sec

Right: Street-fighting in Italy, 1944, with a No. 4 rifle and a Thompson submachine gun.

supplement the Enfield output. It was a solid-frame swing-cylinder revolver based on the well-known Military and Police model, slightly modified to accept the Enfield 200-grain cartridge. It handled much better than the Enfield, and was far more popular as a result, but it was actually less robust and more prone to minor troubles and misfires. The latter occurred because the US ammunition needed a lighter strike than the British, and a dirty mechanism could easily deliver too light a blow. For some reason many of these Smith & Wessons were issued with a low-cut, almost 'quick draw' holster, which added greatly to their reputation, though not much to their practical effectiveness.

There were other American revolvers in service also, all of them bought during the depressing times after Dunkirk when it seemed as though the country would be overwhelmed before it could replace the weapons left on the French beaches. One such purchase was of .45in Smith & Wessons, together with several thousand Colts of the same calibre. Many of these weapons were only issued to special forces, who could be kept separate for ammunition issues. In other cases the revolvers were handed straight to the Home Guard for home defence use only.

There was only one automatic pistol in British service during the war, if one discounts those 'liberated' from the enemy, and this was the Browning 9mm. Originally known as the Model 35, or 'Hi-Power', it was the official side-arm of the Belgian army before the war. In 1939 the drawings were brought to Britain and eventually sent to the firm of John Inglis in Canada, who turned out an order for Chiang Kai Shek's Army in 1943. With no more orders to fulfil, Inglis then made guns for Britain. They were issued to airborne and commando units and became immensely popular because the Browning is a very good pistol indeed. It is strong, reliable, reasonably resistant to dirt – and not all automatic pistols are – and it carried no less than 13 rounds in the large magazine in the butt. The early ones had an elaborate and optimistic backsight which alleged a range of up to 500 yards, together with a large wooden holster, much like that for a Mauser or Parabellum, which clipped to the butt and formed a stock. These fripperies were cut out when serious wartime production got under way, and they are now rare on remaining survivors. The Chinese demanded them on all their order.

The Browning did so well in war service that it was adopted in 1946 as the standard British side-arm and is still so today. One reason for its popularity is the fact that it uses the same ammunition as the submachine guns, and so there were virtually no ammunition supply difficulties, nor any shortages of rounds for training and practice. This was in marked contrast to the unfortunate Enfields.

Hand-Operated Rifles

Britain never put a self-loading rifle into service during the war. For that matter neither did Italy or Japan, but at least these latter two experimented with a few designs. In Britain the prejudices were too strong and the factory space too scarce for much alteration to the established products, whether or not they were the best that could be had. In many

Rifle No. 1 (SMLE)		
Ammunition	.303in SAA	
Length	44.75in	1132mm
Weight unloaded	8lb 2oz	3.71kg
Barrel	25.19in	640mm
Magazine	10-round detachable box	
Muzzle velocity	2200ft/sec	670m/sec

Rifle No. 4

Ammunition	.303in SAA	
Length	44.43in	1128mm
Weight unloaded	9lb 1oz	4.17kg
Barrel	25.19in	640mm
Magazine	10-round detachable box	
Muzzle velocity	2400ft/sec	731m/sec

Below: Men of the Royal Engineers use fixed bayonets as improvised probes during a search for mines in the North Africa campaign in February 1943.

cases second-best had to suffice, and this was nowhere clearer than with the infantryman's best friend, his rifle.

Not that anyone in Britain thought that the Enfield was second-best. It had served well since its introduction in 1895, with some alterations and additions. The most notable of these was the adoption of one size of rifle in 1903 for both cavalry and infantry, and this rifle, known as the Short Magazine Lee-Enfield, or SMLE, was still the service rifle in 1939. It was not declared obsolete or replaced until 1941. The SMLE was undoubtedly an exceptionally good rifle. It used the Lee bolt-action which locked by rear lugs and had a detachable bolt-head which could be changed to compensate for varying head space. The rear lugs allowed a bolt movement of the same length as the cartridge, and no more. A fortuitous design of the locking surfaces gave a particularly easy movement to the bolt handle, and with a little use to rub off the edges, coupled with a light coating of oil, the SMLE bolt was the fastest and lightest in the world. Aimed fire could be undertaken up to 15 rounds a minute without much fatigue by a trained soldier, and that was thought to be more than enough for anyone. It is – but the trouble lies in training the soldier. The fatal error in the use of bolt rifles is the time taken to train soldiers to be proficient. In wartime they never get enough practice and so are never better than average or even bad shots.

With a self-loading rifle the training is easier and quicker, though cleaning and maintenance may take longer. The British War Office took a long time to realize this basic fact, and although designers were encouraged to try and produce a satisfactory British self-loader, the War Office laid down such stringent requirements that none succeeded, and the army went to war in 1939 carrying the same rifle as it had carried in 1918 – often quite literally the same rifle. One other snag with the SMLE was that it took much factory effort to make. During the 1920s an improved design had appeared which kept the best features of the SMLE, but was cheaper and quicker to produce. At the same time the naming was changed, so that the SMLE became the Rifle Number 1, Mark 3 and the new rifle was the Rifle Number 4. Manufacture of the Number 4 started in 1938, and the Number 1 had already virtually ended in Britain, though many were made in Australia until the middle of the war.

The Number 4 (No. 4) had the same bolt, body, barrel and magazine as the No. 1, but there were several simplifications

for manufacture. The wooden stock was the same, but the fore-end changed in outline. The sights were new. On the No. 1 the backsight was an open U and it took time to teach a man to use it properly. On the No. 4 it became an aperture. Later in the war, when production had to be cut to the bone, the aperture had only two settings, for 300 and 600 yards, and there was a complicated formula for using the fixed bayonet to give a correct elevation for the intervening ranges. It was a complete horror and no recruit could ever remember it; after 1944 replacement backsights were issued which allowed a proper graduation for range. Apart from cheaper wood and obvious short-cuts, the No. 4 performed just as well as the old No. 1, though it never had the same 'feel' and quality about it. There was no doubt about it: the No. 1 was an aristocrat, and no other rifle equalled it.

The weak point of the Enfields was the ammunition. The .303in round was already out of date in 1939, but it was kept on for the same reasons as were the rifles – it was too expensive to change and military conservatism could not see the obvious. The .303 had done well in the Boer War and on the Indian frontier; it had done far less well in the Flanders trenches and the Gallipoli hills. A further pointer might have been the difficulties involved in changing the Czech ZB 30 light machine gun to .303, but none of this counted. At least two select committees had condemned the round as being too powerful and out of date, but the stocks were so large, and the cost of re-tooling the factories so great, that it had to go on.

The .303 was a rimmed round, and to avoid jamming the Enfield rifles their clips had to be carefully loaded with the rims lying in just the right places. When they did, reloading was straightforward and firing a delight. But misplace the rims and the bolt stuck on the forward movement – the same happened in the Bren too.

However, despite the shortcomings the British soldier grew to love his bolt-action rifles. Despite the obvious drawbacks to them, very few infantrymen ever picked up a Garand or a G 43 in preference to the Enfield.

The Australian Army continued to carry No. 1 rifles right until the end of the war, by which time they were no longer in service with British forces in Europe. The Indian Army did the same, and these favoured Commonwealth troops were often the envy of the British, who felt they had a slightly poorer weapon in their No. 4s. In this they were mistaken, and the No. 4 still soldiers on today, re-barrelled to the NATO calibre of 7.62mm and used as a sniping rifle.

Jungle warfare brought home the necessity of light equipment and simplicity. Although the Enfields did remarkably well because they were so resistant to rust, mud and rough treatment, they were nevertheless heavy and rather long. It was decided that what was needed was a short carbine firing the same ammunition, a weapon that was light to carry yet gave a good punch. The simple answer seemed to be to cut down the No. 4, and this was done, providing the soldier with the No. 5.

The No. 5 was, to put it mildly, not a success. It was short and light all right, and it looked well with a conical flash-hider on the muzzle, a thick rubber butt pad and a new and rather attractive knife bayonet. The trouble came when it was fired. It had been reduced in weight by 2lb (1kg), and this upset the recoil energy of the rifle completely. Instead of the controllable movement of the No. 4, the jungle carbine had a savage kick, coupled with a much sharper noise that left a ringing sound in the ears. The barrel had been shortened, and this gave a higher pressure at the muzzle and a greater blast. What it needed was a lower-powered round, as its designer must have known, but wartime pressures presumably forced him to ignore ballistic truths, and the result showed that you cannot do that. About 100,000 were made, but not all were issued due to the furiously hostile reports it received, and one assumes that the remainder were decently scrapped. It had the shortest life of any British rifle. It first appeared in May 1945, and was withdrawn in August 1946.

Viewed in retrospect the story of British rifles in World War II is one of no great distinction or innovation. Having set on a design before the war the British continued to produce it as fast as they could, which was never fast enough, until 1945. The rifle itself was out of date before the war began, but it survived because the soldiers overcame its deficiencies largely by training but also by using other weapons in their armoury. There is no doubt that Britain should have followed the lead of other nations and gone for a self-loader as soon as World War I ended.

Submachine Guns

It has been accepted as a matter of historical fact that Britain displayed no interest at all in submachine guns until some time in 1940 or 1941, and then had to build the Sten in a great hurry. But this is a distortion of the truth; in fact there was a good deal of interest in, and work done on, submachine guns from 1916 onwards. The lack of enthusiasm came from the military authorities, and it was totally dampening.

Below: A posed picture of a jungle patrol in Burma during 1944. The troops carry No. 4 rifles and Thompson submachine guns.

The first gun to be tried was the Italian Villar Perosa, followed by the Bergmann MP 18, a captured specimen, and the report on this latter was sent to GHQ in France asking for their opinion of it as a trench-fighting weapon. The reply is interesting since it must be remembered that the Bergmann had been introduced for that very purpose. First of all, GHQ took 11 months to reply, so that it was not hard to deduce that the tone was unlikely to be favourable, and it was not. After a rather specious survey of the requirements of the infantryman's weapon in trench warfare it concludes with the memorable phrase: 'It follows that no weapon of the pistol nature can ever replace the rifle as the infantryman's main arm.' All of which is true, but was quite beside the point in view of the question asked.

From then on the design department at Enfield examined and reported on practically every submachine gun that was made during the last years of World War I and up to 1939. The War Office always seemed to be able to find some good reason for not looking further at them, usually quoting lack of effective range. It must be remembered that despite the experience of the trenches, infantrymen were still expected to engage the enemy at 600 yards (550m) with aimed rifle fire, and the bayonet was the close-range weapon.

In 1932 appeared a phrase that was to be repeated several times in the following year. Reporting on trials of the Finnish Suomi submachine gun, the document says, 'This is probably one of the best "gangster" weapons we have seen', and from then on the idea seems to have stuck that only criminals used submachine guns – proper soldiers had nothing to do with them. In 1938 the BSA Company was told that the War Office was not supporting the buying of Thompson submachine guns made under licence in Britain as 'the British Army is not interested in gangster weapons'. This seems to be the last time that the expression was used in official writing, because soon after that the realization dawned that there are not actually any class rules in war.

The first shock came shortly after the start of the war when patrolling British soldiers found themselves up against the fast-firing MP 38, or more probably the MP 28 and 34, and the first request for a British model was on 22 December 1939.

Some gentlemanly deliberations followed, centring on where best to buy supplies. The Thompson licence had run out at BSA and the parent US firm was fully booked supplying the French! It was assumed, rightly no doubt in view of Finland's war with Russia, that the Suomi was not available. While these weighty matters were being pondered, Dunkirk happened and the situation suddenly became not only desperate but dangerous too. With no foreign manufacturer it was decided right away to copy the best available enemy pattern, and the MP 28 was chosen. The Admiralty took the initiative in this choice, and they agreed to split a first order of 50,000 with the Air Ministry, who wanted the guns for the defence of aerodromes against parachutists. The first prototypes passed all their tests in November 1940 (by which time the main danger was already past) and went into production right away.

This weapon was called the Lanchester after the chief designer, and it was a straight copy of the MP 28, differing only in very small details and in some of the materials used. In the end all the production went to the navy, who still had them in service in the mid-1960s, and they were very much a naval piece of ordnance, being heavy, strong and with the magazine housing made of that material so beloved of sailors – brass. The Lanchester had an undistinguished war, since it was too heavy for marines to use ashore with any enthusiasm, and its main use was for shipboard defence and small landing parties.

The army demanded something simpler and lighter than the Lanchester, and asked for a copy of the MP 38/40, or Schmeisser as it was generally called. The design department of Enfield decided against another slavish copy, but took note of the Schmeisser idea of component manufacture and adapted it to a much simpler design. The result was the STEN gun, the name coming from two initials of the design team and the letters EN from Enfield. It was demonstrated first in January 1941, about eight months after first deciding to make it, and the first production models came off the line in June.

This first model was the Mark I and despite a deliberate attempt to keep frills away it was a little too refined. The

Left: A soldier moves forward with his MK 2 Sten in Italy, 1944. Note the improvised fore-grip for the left hand.

Machine Carbine, 9mm Sten, Mark II		
Ammunition	9mm SAA Ball (9mm Parabellum)	
Length	30in	762mm
Weight unloaded	6lb 8oz	2.95kg
Barrel	7.75in	196mm
Magazine	32-round detachable box	
Cyclic rate	550rpm	
Muzzle velocity	1250ft/sec	381m/sec

Mark II reduced everything to the minimum, and became the widest used of all the marks. In the Mark II there was nothing superfluous at all. The simple box magazine was a direct copy of the MP 38, and held the same 32 9mm Parabellum rounds. The body was a steel tube, the magazine housing a pressing, the stock a piece of tubular steel, and the pistol-grip a steel stamping. The only machined parts were the barrel and bolt, and both were simple. The gun could be made in the simplest machine shop and manufacture was sub-contracted all over the country to garages and rural workshops. Production reached astonishing peaks – one special factory alone turning out over 20,000 a week in 1942 – and the total made was more than two million. BSA made more than 400,000 of the Marks I and II and, all told, probably over 3½ million of all marks were built.

The Mark II had the advantage that it could be dismantled easily, and so was attractive to Resistance fighters in the occupied countries, who carried them around in shopping bags and briefcases, but the Mark III was even simpler. It had a fixed barrel and a one-piece body and barrel casing which cut out several manufacturing processes and brought the time and cost down even further; this model was made in the Long Branch factory in Canada also. It became as common as the Mark II in British service, although it was not exported to the same extent.

Next there were the abortive variants of the Mark IV, intended for parachute use, which had a folding stock and cut-down body, but they were unsuccessful and never introduced. In 1943 a version of the Mark II was produced with a silencer, and it was highly successful and stayed in service for long after the war. It was probably the most widely used silent weapon in the entire war, as it too was given to Resistance fighters all over Europe.

The final version was the Mark V of 1944. It was introduced in an attempt to overcome some of the users' objections to the Marks II and III, which, it was alleged, were unreliable and prone to jamming at critical moments. As a result they gave the gun a number of unflattering names of which 'Stench gun' and 'Woolworth gun' were the kindest. To some extent this criticism held true, since the single-column magazine was by no means good, and slight damage to it could easily affect the feed. The Mark V Sten did not, unfortunately, address this side of the problem as it left the magazine untouched and concentrated on a more robust and better-finished gun. The Mark V was certainly a great outward improvement on the previous marks and handled better too. It had a wooden butt and a wooden forward pistol grip, together with fancier sights. Tolerances were held to closer limits and mechanical reliability was excellent. It was adopted immediately by the airborne forces, and was used in quite large numbers from D-Day onwards. It was only finally phased out in the early 1960s in favour of the Sterling.

From total disinterest in 1939 to virtual domination of design in 1945 is a remarkable performance. The Sten became so well known that its name is still used to denote a

submachine gun, no matter what its real name or nationality. Despite the frequency of jams and a reputation for stopping at the wrong moment, the gun fought on practically every battle front in every theatre. It was copied in clandestine workshops all over Europe, and is still being made, if some intelligence reports are to be believed. It was copied in Germany to arm the so-called Werewolves, and carried by the Vietminh against the French in Indo-China. Almost reluctantly, Britain produced a winner and seemed as bewildered as anyone else at its success.

Machine Guns

On the whole, the British machine-gun story is a sensible and happy one, for the war was started with proven and reliable designs which were in quantity production and few changes were made throughout. The only problem facing the Government was to find sufficient factory space for the numbers of guns required, and there was never the nerve-wracking attempt to develop and produce a new design under the pressures of war expediency. With the British Army, it was either the Bren or the Vickers – saving a few oddities which crept in from time to time.

The Lewis was also to be found in the early years, since there were quite large stocks of it and it fired the .303 round equally as well as the others, but the Lewis had been replaced by the Bren in 1936 and had been withdrawn into the reserve before the war started. After Dunkirk every gun that could shoot was pressed into use, and all the Lewis guns came out again to be put onto armoured cars, lorries and concrete machine-gun posts beside railway lines and along the edges of the beaches. There were Lewis guns of every kind at that time, many of them the stripped aircraft version from the two-seater fighters of the 1920s. As the danger receded most

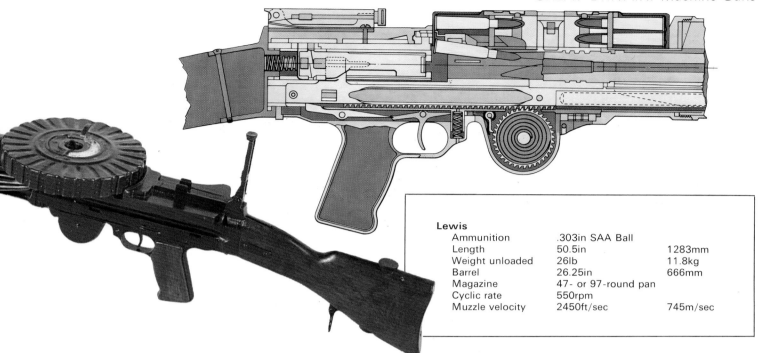

Lewis		
Ammunition	.303in SAA Ball	
Length	50.5in	1283mm
Weight unloaded	26lb	11.8kg
Barrel	26.25in	666mm
Magazine	47- or 97-round pan	
Cyclic rate	550rpm	
Muzzle velocity	2450ft/sec	745m/sec

of them were taken over by the Home Guard, where they continued until 1945. Several hundred others were put onto merchant shipping, particularly coastal ships and fishing vessels, for local protection against dive bombers and low-level strafing in the English Channel and North Sea.

Every now and then the newspapers would carry an encouraging story of a plane being shot down by one of these guns, and there was usually a photo of a smirking gunner standing by a Lewis, striking as casual a pose as he could muster. But in general the Lewis played a minor part in the war, though a necessary one.

The brunt of the fighting was done with the Bren, a

remarkable gun by any standards, the proof of which lies in the fact that it is still in service today, virtually unchanged except for its calibre from the day when it was first adopted in 1935. The story of how it came to be a British gun has been told often enough, for like so many British small arms of this century the Bren is not a native design. It started as the Czechoslovakian ZB 30, which derived from a small family of similar guns going back to the early 1920s, and in 1932 and 1933 it was extensively tested in Britain. The Czechs

Below: Anti-aircraft patrols use Lewis guns on Britain's inland waterways in November 1940.

changed the calibre to .303in and made a few alterations to the gas system of the ZB 30, and the War Office chose it as the Lewis replacement. It was as simple as that; apart from changing the dimensions on the drawings from metric to imperial, little else needed to be done.

Quantity production started in 1938 at Enfield and carried on without a stop for the entire war. The only other factory to make Brens in any number was that of John Inglis in Canada, who turned out an order in 7.92mm Mauser calibre for Chiang Kai Shek in 1942/3, then made .303in versions for the remaining years of the war. At Lithgow in Australia the Government factory made a small number. Otherwise, all Brens came from Enfield, and it is a solemn thought that one good air-raid in 1940 could have brought the entire production to a halt. Apparently there were neither drawings nor jigs held anywhere else in the country!

The Bren is an excellent example of a light machine gun, if not the best that has ever been made. It is reliable, robust, simple and accurate. Add to that the fact that it is remarkably free from stoppages and one can see why it has been held in such affection by the British soldier for nearly 40 years. It is a fairly straightforward gas-operated gun, using the long-stroke principle with a variable size of gas hole in the block. This gas hole can be changed in size simply by rotating the block with the nose of a round, and this only takes a few seconds. The barrel is removable by unlocking a coarse threaded collar at the breech and lifting the barrel away, using the carrying handle; the hand never has to touch a piece of hot metal. Dismantling is uncomplicated, and cleaning relatively easy. It is light enough – 22lb (10kg) – to be carried by one man and could be fired by him from the hip as he advanced. The top-feeding box magazine was in the best place for easy carriage, though it did mean the sights had to be offset to the left and this meant that there were no left-handed Bren gunners.

The only drawback to the gun was that top-feeding box magazine, not because it fed from the top, but because it was the chief source of stoppages. The lips of the magazine were rather vulnerable to damage when being carried in pouches or pockets, and if these lips were bent the ammunition was not presented to the bolt correctly. But perhaps the main culprit was the ammunition in any case. The ZB series had been designed for the rimless Mauser round, and the change to the rimmed .303 brought some troubles that were never properly cured. The rounds had to be loaded with their rims one in front of the other, thus allowing the lower one to slide along with the bolt as it was pushed out forwards. If the rim was behind, either from careless loading or from the magazine being jolted, a stoppage occurred straight away. It was easily corrected, but it was a nuisance.

Another annoyance was that if the magazine was filled to its absolute capacity, or by mistake a bit beyond, it was prone to jam also. It would stick the rounds against the magazine side and not feed any of them. Again, it was easily cured, either by working the bolt by hand to clear a couple of rounds out, or by giving the magazine a good thump.

The Bren served all over the world during the war and about 300,000 were made. It was never an easy gun to build and it took a great deal of machining time, which is expensive in a war. The body, for instance, weighed 4½lb (2.04kg), but it was machined out of a forging weighing 22lb (10kg), and most of the difference in those weights went on the factory floor as swarf and chippings during the 226 operations needed to complete that one component. There were several attempts to simplify the design during the war, but all that was possible was to trim off the frills. From the original Mark I in 1938 to the Mark III and IV in 1944 all that was achieved was a simpler backsight, the loss of a handle and a shoulder strap, non-adjustable bipod legs and a simpler, shorter barrel. One other thing went too – the tripod. All the original Brens had a tripod mounting in their field kit. It was meant to allow fixed-line firing and anti-aircraft firing. It was of little use at either task, and most of the tripods stayed on the beaches at Dunkirk and were never replaced.

The only gun to rival the Bren was the Vickers-Berthier, a design of equal simplicity and reliability which originated

Above: A Bren MK 1 in action in France, 1944.

Bren Mk 2

Ammunition	.303in SAA Ball	
Length	45.25in	11.50mm
Weight unloaded	22lb 5oz	10.15kg
Barrel	25in	635mm
Magazine	30-round detachable box	
Cyclic rate	500rpm	
Muzzle velocity	2400ft/sec	731m/sec

with a Frenchman in 1909, was improved in the early 1920s and bought by Vickers as a commercial venture in 1925. A few small countries took it, but the big step came in 1932 when the Indian Government adopted it for the Indian Army. The procurement of weapons in India was divorced from that of Britain, and different judgement could be used. The VB, as it was known, used almost the same long-stroke gas system as the Bren, and nearly the same locking by means of a tilting breech block. The dimensions were the same, or very close, and so were the magazines and the feed. Indeed, at first glance they are the same, but a second look reveals the differences in outline and contour which show the VB to be a little more graceful and appealing. This difference was even carried to the tripod, where the main members were gently curved.

Below: A Vickers medium machine gun in action during the North African desert campaign. Note the condenser tube leading from the barrel jacket to the condenser can.

But it is not the differences that are startling, it is the similarities; the VB is so like the Bren that one begins to wonder if there was collusion between the designers. It seems unlikely, but even the magazines hold the same number of rounds, and the carrying handles are almost identical. The chief difference lies in the precision of the locking. In the Bren the breech block is forced against the top of the body throughout the entire forward movement, and this extra friction places a top limit on the rate of fire of somewhere about 800 rpm. The VB locked only at the last moment of forward travel, and this fact, together with its slightly lighter moving parts, made it possible to push the rate of fire up to

at least 1,200 rpm. In this fast-firing guise it was called the Vickers Gas Operated (VGO) gun, and was used as an aircraft observer's armament. When aircraft speeds became too high for hand-held guns, some VGOs were taken over by the army, and the Special Air Service (SAS) in particular used them on their jeeps during desert patrols. For this task they had the aircraft 96-round flat drum instead of the box magazine.

In most of the actions fought by the Indian Army in Burma and elsewhere the infantry carried VBs, but they were always described as Brens and never got the credit they deserved. They were manufactured at Ishapore until 1945,

only the first models being built in the Vickers works, and all told probably not more than 30,000 were made.

The other machine gun that was widely used by the British Army was the Vickers, a weapon still held in almost the same awe and reverence as royalty. In 1939 it was already 57 years old, if one makes allowances for slight changes in design, yet there was never the least doubt in deciding that it should continue in service; in fact, so strong was the conviction in the infallibility of the Vickers that the question of replacing it does not seem to have arisen at all. It had performed prodigies in World War I and was confidently expected to go on performing prodigies. To nobody's

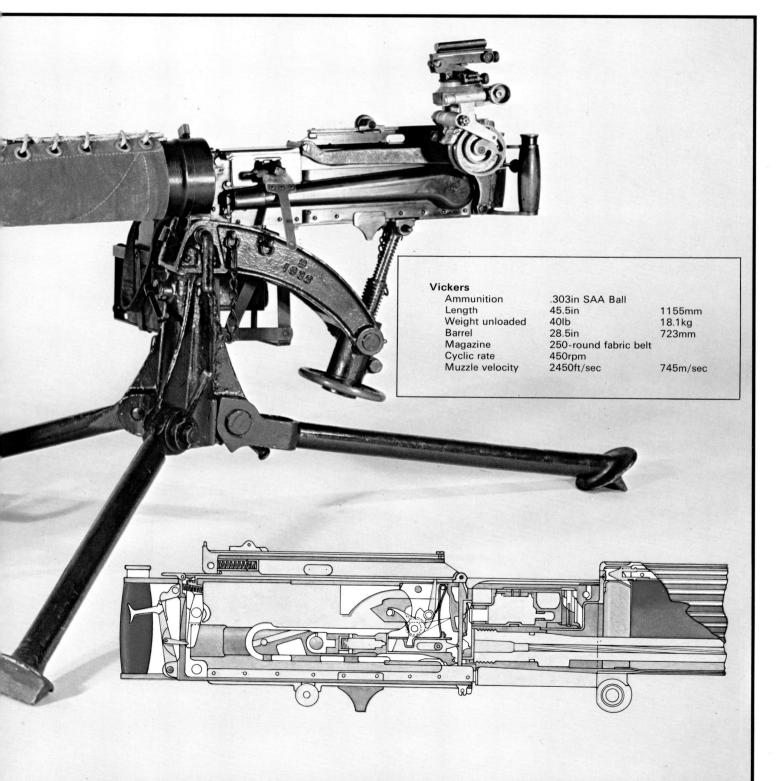

Vickers

Ammunition	.303in SAA Ball	
Length	45.5in	1155mm
Weight unloaded	40lb	18.1kg
Barrel	28.5in	723mm
Magazine	250-round fabric belt	
Cyclic rate	450rpm	
Muzzle velocity	2450ft/sec	745m/sec

surprise it did, and would still do so today.

The Vickers was a lightened Maxim, originally adopted in 1912, but based on the Maxim gun of 1882. It was quite large, heavy, cumbersome and water-cooled. To move it required a gun team of at least three men, preferably more, and it needed two or three men to keep it in action plus plenty of water, some spare barrels and a man to fill extra belts. Given this rather lavish manpower it was capable of providing supporting fire over a distance of 4,000 yards (3,700m) for as long as the ammunition supply lasted. It mattered not to the Vickers if the fire task was measured in minutes, hours or days, the result was always the same – absolute reliability and absolute predictability. Some soldiers almost worshipped it.

Since the workings of the Maxim gun are described under the section devoted to guns of the USSR, we will not repeat it all here. It will be sufficient to say that in the Vickers the lock was turned upside down, thereby saving a good deal of space, and the entire construction was of lighter materials, including some aluminium. The British ammunition was almost identical to the Soviet 1908 round of 7.62mm (.30in) and used the same belt feed. The Vickers gained on its rivals by being light enough for man-carrying, though each load was in the region of 50lb (23kg) and the tripod was a dia-bolical load that one never forgets.

Vickers guns were marshalled into a support platoon, usually of four but sometimes of six guns, under the control of battalion headquarters. They were generally put out in sections of two for their fire tasks, since two guns gave an ideal weight of fire for most tactical situations, and each pair of guns was under the command of a corporal. But there were also machine-gun battalions in which three companies were armed with nothing else but the Vickers, each one having three platoons of six guns, a grand total of 54. In these battalions, and indeed in the infantry battalions as well, the guns were nearly always carried in the universal carrier, one gun to each carrier. It was the only satisfactory way to move the weight of ammunition and supporting equipment that the gun needed.

Airborne forces used the gun too, taking it into action with the main components packed into the leg-bag. In order to carry all the ammunition more men were needed in each platoon, and sometimes their loads were quite horrifying. The author once weighed the leg-bag of a Vickers Number 3 (he carried the water can and some ammunition) and found that he was proposing to go through the door of the plane with 112lb (51kg) on his leg!

Despite the obvious drawbacks of an old water-cooled gun the Vickers stayed in service for 15 years after the war ended, and to the last it confirmed the soundness of the original decision to retain it. The British Army may have entered the war with inadequate weapons in some respects, but in its machine guns there is no doubt that it was on the right lines.

Anti-Tank Rifles

Anti-tank rifles were the fashionable infantry anti-armour weapon in the 1930s. Although the German Mauser showed the way in 1918, nothing much happened until 1934 when the Poles and British both started to develop derivations of the Mauser in order to counter what they saw as an increasing German tank threat. The British rifle owed little to the Mauser in the end, except for the basic idea, for it became a magazine-fed, bolt-action repeater with the magazine feeding from the top. It was a very powerful weapon for its time, firing a .55in (14mm) steel-cored bullet at a muzzle velocity of 3,250ft/sec (990m/sec) which could penetrate any of the then current tanks up to a range of 250m. One must remember that at that time tank armour was little better than it had been in 1918, and a .55in bullet was something for a tank crew to really be wary about. On most tanks it would go straight through the front armour and make a terrible mess inside.

The rifle was developed under the control of the small-arms committee, who called it the 'Stanchion', but the leading light in the design team, one Captain Boys, died just before it

came into service, and as a mark of respect the name was changed to Boys – or rather, Rifle, Anti-tank, .55in Boys, Mark I. It was officially approved on 24 November 1937 and full production started soon after at Enfield and the Birmingham Small Arms Factory (BSA).

The Boys was an all-steel weapon, and the long barrel recoiled along a slide on the butt to absorb the worst of the shock of firing. Even so it was a considerable jolt, and recruits were regaled with grisly stories of the damage that it would do to them. There was a round muzzle-brake, later changed to a flat harmonica type, and a monopod support. Firing it was not as bad as was supposed, except that the noise was ear-shattering. The main requirement – and it applied to all these high-powered rifles, regardless of nationality – was to keep a firm hold of it after pulling the trigger and allow the recoil slide to take the shock. But if the firer loosened his grip (and the deafening crack from the muzzle encouraged him to do so) then the rifle took control and gave him an almighty shove in the shoulder and a bruise that lasted a week, together with a strained neck from the whip-lash effect of the head.

Of all the anti-tank rifles that were used in World War II the Boys was made in the largest numbers. BSA alone made

63,000 before they stopped in 1942, and lesser quantities were produced in Enfield and by the Inglis factory in Canada. The rifle was the basic platoon anti-tank defence of most of the Commonwealth countries, and in 1940 it was also put onto armoured cars. The makeshift vehicles which defended the British airfields during the Battle of Britain generally carried a few Boys rifles in each unit, and in the Western Desert the ex-World War I Rolls Royce armoured cars which patrolled the Cyrenaica border carried a Boys in the turret alongside the machine gun. In fact the Desert was probably the most successful place for the Boys, since it could defeat the light Italian tanks without too much trouble. In France and Norway it was less effective, due to the thicker armour then coming in on German tanks, and its last worthwhile action was probably in Malaya in early 1942 when two Japanese light tanks were knocked out at a roadblock by the 1/14th Punjabis.

In early 1942, when the invasion of Tunisia was being planned, the airborne troops had no anti-tank defence at all and an experiment was tried with a cut-down Boys. About 6in (15cm) was cut off the barrel in order to get it into a parachute container, and the first models did away with the muzzle-brake. It was a failure. The shorter barrel sharply reduced the velocity, and so the penetration, which was by no means adequate at the best of times for 1942, and the loss of the muzzle-brake made it an appalling weapon to fire. A few were actually taken to Tunisia and tried with no effect at all, and the troops quickly dumped them. Fortunately the Projector, Infantry, Anti-Tank (PIAT) came shortly afterwards, just in time.

Rifle, Anti-Tank, .55in, Boys Mk 1 and Mk 2		
Ammunition	.55in Boys	
Length	63.5in	1614mm
Weight unloaded	36lb	16.32kg
Barrel	36in	915mm
Magazine	5-round detachable box	
Muzzle velocity	3250ft/sec	900m/sec
Armour penetration	21mm at 300m at 90°	

FRANCE

Every nation seems to have quite definite individual characteristics in its national products, and this comes through quite clearly in military equipment. In France the majority of industrial and domestic articles are noteworthy for being robust, simple, logical, and usually ugly. The same trend appears in French infantry weapons. No other country could have produced a rifle quite as ungainly as the MAS 36, yet in its way it was as practical, economical and reliable as that extraordinary corrugated pony cart of the 1950s, the Citroen 2 CV. The most compelling factor in French weapons was finance, or rather lack of finance, for there was never enough to go round, and in the inter-war years there was less than ever. A combination of socialist pacifism and the defensive theories of M. Maginot ensured that the defence budgets of successive governments went into concrete rather than weapons and ammunition, and the languor that accompanies victory replaced the energy and vigour that is needed for effective readiness against aggression. It was so everywhere in Europe, but nowhere so pronounced as in France.

The French Army was well aware of what it needed, but at its wit's end to get it. In the field of infantry weapons the first and most crying need was for a new round of small-arms ammunition. The 8mm Lebel had scarcely survived the First World War, and was obviously hopelessly inadequate for any other. It suffered from the appalling defect that it was designed for a tubular magazine, and so had to have a large flat base to ensure that the point of one bullet did not strike the ignition cap in the base of the cartridge directly in front. This could only be done by making a large difference in diameter between the two, and the resulting conical cartridge case was extremely difficult to fit into a box magazine. This is nowhere more vividly shown than in the Chauchat light machine gun, where the magazine practically describes a semicircle under the gun.

Luckily, there was just enough money to design and manufacture a new round, and so the long-lived 7.5mm model of 1924/29 came into being – it is still in service. Lack of finance forced the long development time on the designers, but it was completed in good time for World War II, though the wretched Lebel continued to soldier on, probably for no better reason than that it could use up left-over 8mm stocks.

A curiosity of French small arms is that there was by 1939 no really effective medium machine gun. The Hotchkiss Model 1914 had done well enough in World War I but there had been more than enough defects and troubles with it, not the least lying in the out-dated strip feed which only Japan copied, and probably regretted. Alone among the combatants France had no belt-fed gun, which is surprising. The Chatellerault light gun was quite adequate, but the lack of suitable medium back-up seems to have stemmed from the fortress theory again. If there was going to be no open

warfare, then there was no need for a mobile medium gun, and the heavy Hotchkiss could stay inside the concrete bunker. If this is a libel, at least it seems to have plenty of circumstantial evidence to support it, and there can be few other explanations so obvious.

From the rather selfish view of the small-arms student, it may seem a pity that the French equipment did not get a chance to really show its worth in the war, though Frenchmen might well not agree. However, it is difficult to give a balanced judgement on the effectiveness of the French equipment since it only had a short opportunity to prove itself in action. After May 1940 there was no further development or improvement in the designs, even where manufacture still continued. Nevertheless, it is possible to see the weaknesses of the weapons which the French Army had to carry

in 1939. Probably the greatest one is the fact that, almost without exception, they were designed in state arsenals under the direction and approval of a committee. There was minimal influence from the specialist gun trade, and government design establishments tend to be less innovative and venturesome than private industry. When they are controlled by committees almost all initiative is squashed.

The result of this attitude to design becomes clear when one looks at the Berthier and MAS rifles, which were undistinguished in the extreme and ugly to boot. It is interesting that none were ever made into sporting rifles. Then compare them with the MAS 1935 pistol, a design which originated in private industry (even if it is a copy of the Colt). This is a clean, sound and workmanlike weapon which would still be in service today if it were not for the fact that it had to fire the 7.5mm French cartridge. The same disadvantage severely shortened the life of the otherwise practical submachine gun, the MAS 38. There are times when one wonders if the French designers were determined to isolate their weapons entirely from any contact with other countries' products. Another question is why there was never a French anti-tank rifle. Whatever may have been the weaknesses of these weapons they were not apparent in the mid 1930s, and indeed the Spanish Civil War gave them quite a boost. But France never tried even one, preferring instead the equally ineffective, yet more expensive and complicated Hotchkiss 25mm gun.

Yet, as we know, there has always been a huge fund of talent and skill in France – and today there is more than ever. It was as strong in the 1920s as it has ever been, but the final verdict must be that crippling financial restrictions and a determination to keep away from future wars was reflected in the military arms supply, and a brave and stout army was committed to battle with obsolete and inefficient weapons which were unworthy of the men who handled them. It is a lesson for us all.

Below: Members of the Maquis 'somewhere in France', 1944. They are equipped with Lebel rifles, Berthier carbines, Sten guns, M1 rifles, and a Colt pistol.

Modèle D'Ordonnance 1892		
Ammunition	8mm cartouche Mle 1892	
Length	9.36in	236mm
Weight unloaded	1lb 14oz	.84kg
Barrel	4.60in	117mm
Magazine	6-round cylinder	
Muzzle velocity	750ft/sec	228m/sec

As with any country which wins a major war, France in the 1920s suffered from the tendency to cut back on all armament expenditure and firmly discourage any attempt to introduce new weapons. The attitude was that what was good enough for the Great War was good enough for anything likely to come in peace-time, and so the old models could go on in service. Although this rule was relaxed for rifles and machine guns, it held fairly well for pistols and little money was forthcoming for any new weapons. The army continued to use the wartime veterans.

Chief among these survivors was the 1892 model revolver, the Modèle D'Ordonnance. It was the official French side-arm throughout the first war, although there were never enough of them to equip more than a proportion of the army, much less the navy and air force. The Modèle D'Ordonnance was a typical late-nineteenth-century military revolver in every way – large, robust and relatively simple in construction. It was solid-framed, with a swing-out cylinder which tipped to the right, a most unusual arrangement. Strangely, the release button for the cylinder was also on the right, making the entire weapon ideal for left-handed shooters but much less convenient for right-handers.

Another peculiarity was that the left side-plate of the lock swung forward, taking the trigger-guard with it and exposing the lock work. For cleaning and general maintenance this was most useful, though it must have offered more openings for dirt to get in than was strictly necessary. The ammunition was a special 8mm cartridge which was unfortunately underpowered in comparison with its contemporaries, so by 1939 the entire weapon was well out of date and little more than an anachronism. But it remained in service until 1945, when it was quietly dropped.

The only real advance made in French military pistols occurred in 1935 when the chief designer of the Société Alsacienne de Construction Mècanique (SACM) produced a new automatic pistol which the Government adopted for military use. The basis was the Colt M 1911A1, and this highly successful model was improved in several small ways internally, leaving the outward appearance little changed. The calibre was altered to take a special French cartridge, the 7.65mm Long. No other country adopted this cartridge, which detracted from its military worth, but the pistol was a good design in all other respects and the army took it as the Modèle 1935A, later adding the Modèle 1935S in which minor changes were made to the recoil spring and locking rib.

The Modèle 35 was needed in such numbers that manufacture was farmed out to other firms and also to the Arsenal

MAS 1935A		
Ammunition	7.65mm Long	
Length	7.45in	189mm
Weight unloaded	1lb 10oz	.73kg
Barrel	4.3in	109mm
Magazine	8-round detachable box	
Muzzle velocity	1000ft/sec	305m/sec

Above: At a road block in France, 1944. The member of the Maquis in the left foreground carries a Lebel revolver, while the one at right has a MAS 35A.

of St Etienne, and this establishment gave its initials to the later models which became the MAS 35, and are known as such today. This automatic pistol was the standard one of the French forces until the German occupation in 1940. By then there were a few in the colonies, but most were in France and were taken into German service, though some were allowed to be retained by the Vichy police. In 1945 quite large numbers were recaptured and the MAS 35 once more became a French military weapon, serving in Indo-China and Algeria until quite recent years. While never outstanding in performance or reputation, the MAS 35 was as good as many others in its time, and perhaps it deserved a better fate.

Although the official-issue pistols were limited to the two models just described, there were many other ones in service, left over from World War I. In 1915 the French Army found that it had far too few pistols for its conscripts, and there was no hope of making sufficient in France, so the gun makers of Eibar in Spain were given a specification for a simple blow-back automatic pistol based on the Browning patents. The calibre was specified as 7.65mm (.30in), which is rather small for military needs, but apparently it sufficed for trench warfare and many thousands were turned out in Eibar – so many in fact that the remaining records are hopelessly inaccurate. When the war ended and the orders ceased abruptly, the firms faced ruin. They therefore continued to make pistols,

in cut-throat competition with each other, until the Spanish Civil War stopped them entirely.

The basic pistol which started all this industry was generally called the Ruby, and large numbers were kept by individual officers until 1940, for the light and handy Ruby was preferred to the heavier revolver and MAS 35. Few officers actually expect to have to use their pistols anyway. Things have got badly out of hand when the officers have to take a part in the fire-fight, and the French military authorities were prepared to take a fairly relaxed view of individual weapons. Other were less charitable, and a 1945 Allied intelligence pamphlet, describing the Ruby, firmly said 'this is not a practical military weapon'!

Hand-Operated Rifles

In the flush of military inventions in the latter part of the nineteenth century France was well to the fore, producing something novel and practical in every field, and not least in respect of explosives – for it was a Frenchman who first made a smokeless propellant. The first brass cartridges were filled with compressed gunpowder simply because there was no other suitable propellant. As a result, any attempt at rapid fire by large bodies of troops masked the entire front in clouds of white smoke and on a still day it was some time before it cleared and allowed the firers to see what they were shooting at. But in the early 1880s a French chemist developed a way of using modified gun-cotton instead of black powder, and the French Army built a special rifle to take advantage of this innovation.

Black powder was a low-order propellant and needed a fairly large cartridge and a slow-moving bullet to get the full use of the energy. Barrels fouled up quickly and the powder was highly susceptible to damp. So the new propellant was a significant step forward, since it avoided all these drawbacks.

The new French rifle was the model 1886, soon called the Lebel after Colonel Lebel, the leader of the military commission which accepted it. There was one novel feature in it, the calibre. The Lebel was the first small-calibre rifle ever to

clothing. To reduce this hazard it was very short, and so not easy to grasp or turn. It had to be turned until it was vertical before it unlocked its two front locking lugs, and then pulled back along a rather tight slide. The reverse action fed in a round and locked it again. It was not a bolt that lent itself to rapid fire, nor did it take kindly to a little battlefield dirt or mud. In fact most firers found it easier to lower the rifle to re-load, and so any attempt at fast shooting produced flailing elbows and waving muzzles.

But the main feature of the old Lebel was in the feed, for it was one of the last of the tubular magazines. The rounds were loaded into a tube which ran along under the barrel and inside the fore-stock, whence they were pushed backwards by a spring. To load the rifle, rounds were fed in one by one in front of the open bolt and pushed into the open end of the tube, against the power of the spring. It was not an operation which could be done in a hurry, nor was it easy

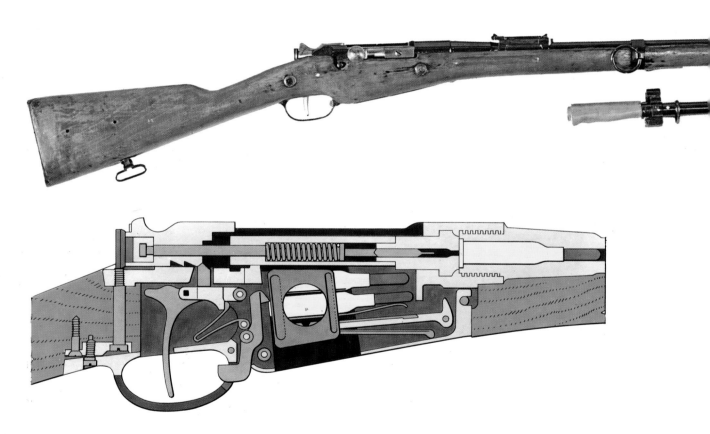

be built in quantity; it was also the first military rifle to use smokeless powder. Apart from these two aspects, the Lebel was very much a re-hash of the two existing French rifles, the black-powder Gras and Kropatschek of 1884. It was therefore very much a nineteenth-century weapon in its conception. It is important to keep this in mind when examining it, for it stayed in service for over 60 years, yet by comparison with its contemporaries it was out of date before the turn of the century.

The Lebel worked by a bolt action, but a rough and awkward bolt. The stubby handle stuck out horizontally, exactly where it was best placed to catch in equipment and

with cold fingers. In fact it was desperately slow and awkward and it was not an operation of modern war at all. Even in 1900 most armies were carrying a rifle which could be loaded with a clip or a charger into a box magazine.

Surprisingly, the Lebel stayed in service throughout World War I, but even more surprisingly it was still in service in substantial numbers in 1939, although there were by then quite serious moves to replace it. The Lebel may have been the latest thing in infantry weaponry in 1886, but it was little better than an interesting anachronism by World War II. Yet it hung on and on and was still being carried in some of the ex-French colonies 15 years after the war ended.

Its actual war service was quite varied. It fought the German Blitzkrieg in 1940, armed the Vichy troops in unoccupied France, was used against the British in Syria and the Japanese in Indo-China, was adopted by the German Army as a second-line reserve arm, and was occasionally used by the French underground movement. Not a bad record for an antique.

Fusil d'Infanterie Modèle 1907 Transformé 1915 (Berthier 07/15)

Ammunition	8mm Cartouche Mle 86	
Length	51.24in	1303mm
Weight unloaded	8lb 6oz	3.79kg
Barrel	31.4in	798mm
Magazine	3-round integral box	
Muzzle velocity	2350ft/sec	716m/sec

Alongside the Lebel was another elderly design, the Berthier, which had been adopted in 1890 as a modernized Lebel. Even at that early stage it had been realized in France that the tubular magazine was dead for military use, and the Berthier was an attempt to put a box magazine underneath a modified Lebel. In 1935 the stocks of Berthiers were re-barrelled to 7.5mm and the magazine changed to a five-shot Mauser type. Even that was derisory for the type of war foreseen at that time, but money was scarce in France in the 1930s and it had to do.

To be fair to the Berthier, it was an improvement on the Lebel. It still retained the incredibly clumsy and rather complicated bolt, but the handle was lengthened and turned over so that it lay more snugly down the right-hand side of the receiver, where it was less likely to catch on things, and its extra length made it easier to handle. The box magazine could be loaded with a clip and it took the modern 7.5mm round, which was a great improvement on the old 8mm Lebel. The greatest drawback to the 8mm was its large flat rim, specially made so that when the rounds were in the tube magazine they lay in a staggered line to prevent the danger of the point of one bullet piercing the percussion cap of the one in front. While this is ideal for tubes, it makes it impossible to put this type of ammunition into a box magazine without running the risk of jams every few shots. That is

Below: Anti-tank gunners struggle up a hill early in the war, carrying Berthier 1892/16 carbines.

exactly what happened to the Berthier when it was first tried, hence the change to 7.5mm and the expense of re-barrelling. Berthiers came in two sizes, rifles and carbines. Infantry units carried the rifles and the artillery and service units the carbines, but carbines were also issued to specialist troops such as machine gunners (who cannot have welcomed the weight and size of it) and drivers. In the French colonial armies where there were still plenty of horses, the cavalry had carbines exclusively.

The Berthiers were in use throughout the war, in the same ways as the Lebel; they too were taken into limited

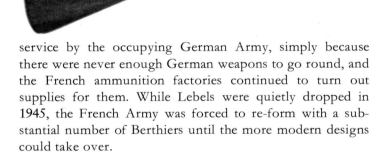

MAS 36		
Ammunition	7.5mm Cartouche Mle 29	
Length	40.15in	1020mm
Weight unloaded	8lb 5oz	3.78kg
Barrel	22.6in	573mm
Magazine	5-round integral box	
Muzzle velocity	2700ft/sec	823m/sec

service by the occupying German Army, simply because there were never enough German weapons to go round, and the French ammunition factories continued to turn out supplies for them. While Lebels were quietly dropped in 1945, the French Army was forced to re-form with a substantial number of Berthiers until the more modern designs could take over.

One of the modern designs was the MAS 36 – in fact it was the only design which was brought in to replace the elderly Berthiers and Lebels. It has the dubious distinction of being the last bolt-action rifle to be adopted by any army in the Western world, and possibly in the whole world. The French had realized as early as 1916 that their 8mm cartridge was poor, but, trapped in the usual economic vice, they had had to go on making it and using it. However, in the 1920s the Government was forced to give up a little money for development of new weapons, and the 7.5mm cartridge resulted. The MAS was the rifle designed to fire it. It first saw the light of day in 1932 at St Etienne and adopted its name from there – Manufacture d'Armes de Saint-Etienne, or MAS. Essentially it was the simplest possible rifle that could be produced in quantity without having to drastically alter the factory, yet at the same time was robust and reliable. Experience with the jams caused by the 8mm ammunition made reliability a key feature of the requirement, and certainly the MAS was, and still is, reliable. It achieved this virtue by losing several others, among them style, grace, smoothness of operation and some degrees of safety.

It was one of the ugliest rifles ever to be made, and one of the least satisfactory to use, for the designer was more interested in the factory foremen than in the firer. The bolt retained the full quarter-turn action for locking and unlocking,

but it was even more inconveniently placed than on the Berthier. For the MAS the locking lugs were put at the rear of the bolt, just as on the Lee-Enfield, and this made the bolt itself longer, so that the handle came well back behind the action and in a most awkward place for the firer's hand to grasp it. It was therefore bent forward to bring the knob above the trigger and this is the unique recognition feature of the MAS. Like the Lebel the butt and fore-end were in two parts, attached to each end of the receiver, and a thin spike bayonet was lodged in a tube under the fore-end. This bayonet was carried reversed in its tube, out of sight, until needed, when it could be pulled out and locked in position. It added a bit to the weight, but saved a separate bayonet scabbard and carrier on the man's equipment, so it was probably an advantage. It depends really on how important the user believes his bayonet to be. A grave drawback to the normal infantryman is that spike bayonets are absolutely useless for such necessary domestic tasks as opening tins and splitting firewood.

The MAS was in service in small numbers for the Battle of France, and served on with the Vichy forces. Production continued at a fairly slow pace throughout the war at St Etienne, some of the output going to the Germans for use on the Atlantic Wall and the western coast. Because these rifles were made from new for the Wermacht they were stamped with the German eagle, which was not usually done with other types commandeered from French stocks.

Although the MAS did not have a particularly distinguished war, it was kept on after 1945 and took part in the fighting in Indo-China and Algeria and is still a reserve store and a standard issue to the police.

Submachine Guns

France, like Britain, the USA and a few more otherwise sensible nations, ignored the submachine gun as an infantry weapon despite the clear indications given by the German and Italian successes with it in World War I. However, the Saint Etienne arsenal tried an experimental design in 1935 and was allowed to develop it on a low priority for a couple of years. The resulting gun appeared at just the right time in the pre-war rush to equip the French Army, and was adopted as a specialist weapon for assault troops, commando operations, patrols and also for the security police, the Garde Mobile.

The MAS 38 showed several characteristics which were sadly lacking in other designs in Europe. It was light, handy and quite accurate; it was fairly resistant to mud and dirt; it was meant to be used for shooting at short range, and nothing else. Far too many of the contemporary submachine guns tried to be all things together, with bayonets on the muzzle, often a bipod, a long wooden stock and sights

reading up to 1,000m. They were heavy, clumsy, and quite incapable of carrying out more than half of the optimistic tasks their designers had set for them. The little MAS avoided all this, and looked quite elegant into the bargain, though it has always been distinguished by its unusual 'crook back' appearance.

The odd shape stems from the barrel being slightly angled to the body and butt. These two latter are in line so that the bolt and spring can run back into the hollow butt, and so save space. In order to keep the sight line low on top of the body, the barrel had to run off at an angle and this meant that the face of the bolt had to be machined to the same angle to meet the breech. At first sight it seems utterly wrong to run a bolt at an angle to a barrel, but in fact it works perfectly well and the cartridge cases don't mind a bit. The MAS was a pleasant little weapon to fire and the saddest thing about it is that it had to be chambered for the 7.65mm Long pistol cartridge, which no other nation has ever used, nor is likely to.

Apart from the shape there were one or two other small inventions on the gun. The bolt could be locked in either the forward or the rear position by pushing the trigger *forwards,* which was a neat way of providing a safety, and the cocking handle opened a dust cover when pulled back. The MAS was

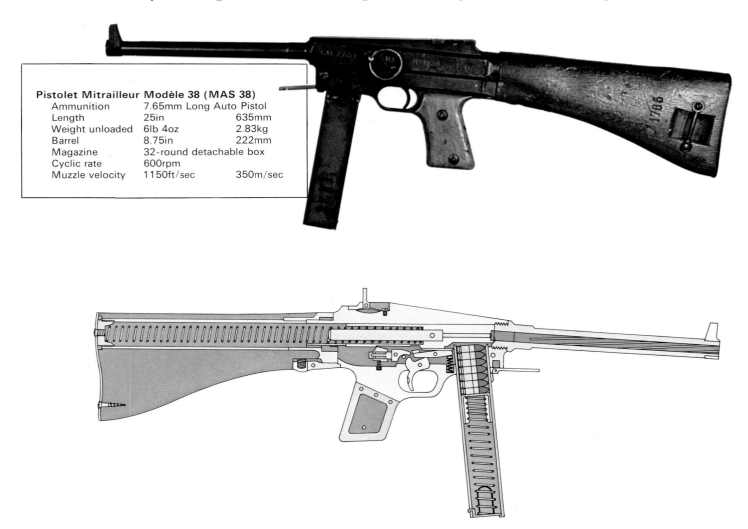

Pistolet Mitrailleur Modèle 38 (MAS 38)

Ammunition	7.65mm Long Auto Pistol	
Length	25in	635mm
Weight unloaded	6lb 4oz	2.83kg
Barrel	8.75in	222mm
Magazine	32-round detachable box	
Cyclic rate	600rpm	
Muzzle velocity	1150ft/sec	350m/sec

a most effective design, and it stands as an example of the standards that could be reached by the arsenal designers if they were not burdened by committees or financial clamps.

Although adopted in 1938 there were few in service before the spring of 1940, and there are almost no accounts of their use in the Battle of France. The arsenal continued to manufacture the gun throughout the war, mainly for police use, and it was used extensively in the campaigns in Indo-China in the late 1940s. Many of those weapons stayed there, and reappeared in Vietnam. Some were still in the original calibre, but many were re-barrelled by the Vietnamese, or even bored through again, to take other ammunition.

Machine Guns

The French mania for economy in defence matters shows up more clearly in their machine guns than in almost any other area. It was not entirely the fault of the military staff; they had known in 1919 that the Chauchat had failed them utterly in World War I and had been responsible for several serious losses in morale as well as casualties. As early as 1920 there was a design for a light machine gun, and the first model appeared in the next year. For three years the development continued slowly, almost at snail's pace, but by 1924 there was a workmanlike and useful prototype undergoing trials.

One major failing of the old Chauchat had been the fact that it had to use the 8mm Lebel ammunition, which was quite unsuited to being fired from an automatic weapon. The State arsenals, short of money and short of time, looked for successful rounds to adapt and they ended with a compromise between the 7.92mm Mauser and the Swiss 7.5mm Rubin. The calibre was 7.5mm and it was by no means entirely successful at first. However, a second version, introduced in 1929, had a modified primer and a better propellant, which enabled it to be 4mm shorter overall. This meant that all the early machine guns that had been built to take the 1924 round had to be withdrawn for modification, but there were no objections since one of the failings of the first series of ammunition had been a tendency to damaging breech explosions, and some firers had been injured.

The machine gun came to be known as the Chatellerault, from the arsenal of that name, and it was broadly based on the Browning Automatic Rifle, with a slight admixture of Berthier features. It was a fairly standard gas-operated weapon which locked the breech block by swinging it up into recesses in the top of the body, much the same as did the BAR, but fired it by a fixed firing pin on a pedestal on the piston, a similar way to the Czech ZB series of light guns. The gas system could be adjusted to regulate the rate of fire. Although it was a little heavy, it gave less trouble than many other designs.

A feature peculiar to the Chatellerault was the provision of two triggers, again a method of saving cost at the expense of

Chatellerault Modèle 24/29

Ammunition	7.5mm Cartouche Mle 24/29	
Length	42.6in	1082mm
Weight unloaded	20lb 4oz	9.24kg
Barrel	19.7in	500mm
Magazine	25-round detachable box	
Cyclic rate	500rpm	
Muzzle velocity	2700ft/sec	823m/sec

weight. The forward trigger fired single shots, and the rear one automatic fire. The arrangement was simple in the extreme, though clumsy since the forward trigger is a bit too far away from the pistol grip for comfort, and it is distinctly awkward for a firer with a small hand.

The vertical box magazine held 30 rounds, which was quite adequate for a platoon and section machine gun, but because the infantry companies only had the heavy Hotchkiss to support them an attempt was made to give the Chatellerault a wider scope by fitting a monopod under the butt. The idea behind this was to allow the gun to be laid on fixed lines for defensive fire tasks – a negation of the purpose of a

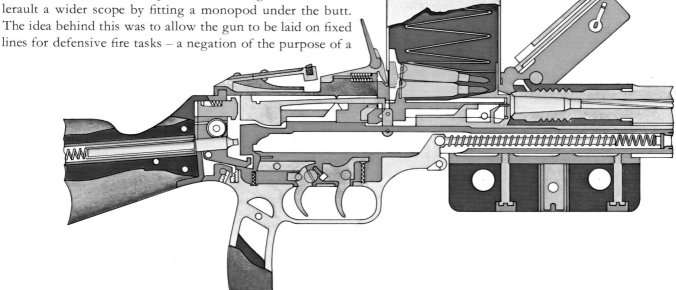

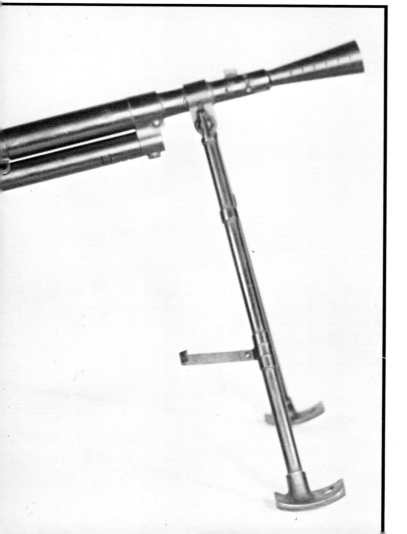

Above: The Chatellerault machine gun in use in the Alps. After the war it was used in Algeria and Indo-China.

light machine gun – and it failed completely, for the whole gun moves far too much when fired to allow for any accuracy.

Driven by the insistent need to save money, the Chatellerault was adopted for vehicle mounting and for so-called fortress mountings. As a vehicle gun it was given a huge ammunition drum carrying 150 rounds, and weighing no less than 10lb (4.5kg) when empty. As the vehicle version of the gun weighed 36lb (16.3kg) without ammunition, the drum was a hefty addition. It was carried vertically on either side of the body, and cannot have been welcomed in the cramped interior of a tank turret.

The same gun was put into the Maginot Line as a 'Fortress' gun, but it was given a unique method of additional cooling for the barrel. Realizing that the guns in the casements might need to fire for long periods, and not having the ability to change the barrel, the designers gave them a peculiar and complicated water injection arrangement which squirted a small jet of cold water straight into the chamber after the cartridge case had been withdrawn. How much heat this jet extracted was not revealed, but the French claimed that it enabled them to fire continuous bursts with no regard for barrel heating at all. Unfortunately they were never given the chance to prove it in action since the Germans were astute enough to come round the back of the forts.

So much for the Chatellerault, which in its original light form was by no means a bad gun. After the war it was used with considerable success in Indo-China and Algeria until replaced by the AA 52 in the mid-1950s. A strong sales

Hotchkiss Modèle 1914		
Ammunition	8mm Cartouche Mle 86	
Length	50in	1270mm
Weight unloaded	52lb	23.58kg
Barrel	30.5in	775mm
Magazine	24- or 30-round metal strips	
Cyclic rate	600rpm	
Muzzle velocity	2380ft/sec	725m/sec

Above: A 1914 Hotchkiss, captured by the Germans from the French in 1940 and recaptured by the British in 1944.

campaign in the 1930s persuaded several small armies to buy it, so it was met in many parts of the world, and may still be.

The support gun for the infantry company was the elderly Hotchkiss, a relic of the early years of the century. Although the Hotchkiss had done quite well in World War I it was out of date in 1939, but, as always, there had been no money to design another, and it had to soldier on. It was big and heavy, but not much more so than the Browning or the Vickers, and being air-cooled it did not need the encumbrances of water cans and condenser tubes, but it had one fatal deficiency in the feed. This was by thin flat strips, a feature of Hotchkiss machine guns since their very beginning, and it was always a source of trouble in action. The flat strip had clips punched in it, and these held the rounds. Each strip took 30 rounds, though there was a long semi-belt made up of jointed three-round sections. However, neither was at all reliable and both were highly susceptible to casual damage.

It is strange that a proper canvas belt was never fully developed for this gun. No other belt would have done, for the ammunition was the 8mm Lebel, and it was never changed until the end of the gun's life. The Hotchkiss gained no benefit from the 7.5mm introduction of 1929.

The German occupying forces were apparently not much interested in the Hotchkiss, and though they were ready enough to use the Chatellerault in their defensive works, in particular along the Atlantic Wall, there are few reports of Hotchkiss being installed. By 1945 the old Hotchkiss had had its day, and very few were retained in service in France. All told the machine gun story had not been a happy one in World War II, and the French Army was ready to take up new designs better suited to their purposes.

SOVIET RUSSIA

To explain Soviet small arms it is necessary to explain something of the Soviet homeland and character, for both these factors acted on the design and the manufacture of the weapons used by the Soviet Army. Throughout its history Russia was well behind the Western nations in general technology and engineering capacity, though there were inventors enough. When the Western nations were expanding their engineering and manufacturing base in the middle and late nineteenth century, Russia was lagging far behind. There was very little light engineering, and not much heavy either, although this was changed as the railways expanded.

The great arsenals of Tula and Kovrov did not begin to make any weapons until the 1890s. Before that all Russian armaments were bought abroad, often from Belgium and the USA. Rifle manufacture started in 1894, and machine guns were first made in 1905, but there was no significant production of any small arms until the early 1920s, when the Communist regime decided that it had to cease to rely on foreign firms and set up a strong national arms industry. One of the first steps was to establish a small-arms design office in 1924 in the Kovrov Machine Gun Factory. The chief of this was Vladimir Fedorov, who in 1916 had designed what is now recognized as the first successful self-loading rifle in the world. This had not been fully developed, and the unsatisfactory 6.5mm round chosen for it had been a poor choice. However, Federov chose as his assistant Vasily Degtyarev, who was to make his name well known within a very few years.

The design office was followed four years later in 1928 with a vigorous manufacturing plan based within the first of several Five Year Plans for the expansion of industry throughout the USSR. The modern Russian arms industry dates from this first plan, and it was only at that time that a

Below: Germans surrender to Soviet troops armed with PPSh-41 submachine guns and Moissin Nagant rifles.

serious attempt was made to design and build weapons in the boundaries of the Soviet Union without the help of other nations. The efforts of that small design office, which of course soon expanded enormously, led to the distinctive and effective weapons which the Red Army used to defeat the German invasion of their country. In the longer term, it led to the uncounted millions of Soviet weapons which have flooded the Eastern world and advanced the cause of Communism since 1945.

The outstanding features of all Soviet small arms are their general coarseness of finish when compared to Western weapons of the same period, and the overall simplicity of the designs. The factories were not capable of devoting too much time or effort to finishing off surfaces to high standards of smoothness, nor is it strictly necessary. While all items which needed it were machined, often to quite fine limits, where it did not matter far less attention was paid to cosmetic effects. The result was that Western observers were apt at first to dismiss Soviet equipment as crude and unsatisfactory, but the Germans soon found that this was not the case.

The Soviet designer had to allow for an overstretched factory with elderly and unsophisticated machines and tools. Hence it was no good designing weapons which could only

be made in quantity on automatic lines. When the Germans invaded in 1941 there were three factories producing machine guns in the USSR, at Tula, Kovrov and Izhevsk. As the war-front rolled eastwards both Tula and Kovrov had to be evacuated and all their machinery moved further east. Exactly what effect these moves had on the production of guns the Russians have never revealed, but it must have been catastrophic for at least a year. Yet not only were the two factories successfully put to work again in their new locations, but two more new ones were built and fitted out at the same time. Some of the machine tools must have been obtained under the Lend-Lease plan from the USA, for Soviet output could not possibly have coped with demands of that size.

The designer also had to contend with straightforward materials, for Russia could not produce much in the way of steel other than the relatively low-stressed varieties. Thus the dimensions of Soviet weapons were generous, and when an attempt was made to reduce the weight, as with the Simonov and Tokarev self-loading rifles, it usually ended in breakages and trouble. It was no accident that the Russian Maxim was the heaviest of any nationality; to maintain the Maxim reputation for reliability, it had to be heavy. But such insistence on simplicity and strength brought its own difficulties too. Quite often the automatic weapons suffered from large bearing surfaces which generated too much friction and stuck in the winter cold when the oil froze, or over-reacted to the vagaries of the ammunition. Generosity with weight in the working parts usually leads to a slow rate of fire and a need for strong springs and trigger sears.

The Soviet designer also had to allow for an unsophisticated user who might not have had much training, and who would need to use the weapon in the most atrocious weather conditions where the weapon could be in below-zero temperatures for weeks on end, covered in snow and dirt, dropped in mud and rarely cleaned. Not for nothing did the PPSh-41 have a chromium-plated barrel liner; Georg Shpagin knew that it would only be pulled through on rare occasions.

Next the designer had to allow for huge quantities in manufacture; the Soviet Army numbered millions of men, and it needed weapons on the same scale. This again led to simplicity in design, and also to as few parts as possible. Spares supply was a vast problem and the fewer there were, and the simpler they fitted, the better. Once a design had been accepted and put into service it was likely to remain in use for some time, as it cost too much to change it. Hence the fact that although the old Moissin Nagant bolt-action rifle was out of date in the 1930s, it paid to keep it on until 1945; likewise the PPSh-41, which was certainly outclassed to a small extent by the PPS-43, but was kept on because it was too much trouble to change. As with many other things in Russia, sheer volume overcame technical considerations almost every time. The result was that the Soviet Army had fewer variations of specific weapons in service than any other army in the war. Once the wheels of the factories had started to turn, it was difficult to stop them, so it paid the designer to be right from the start.

Pistols

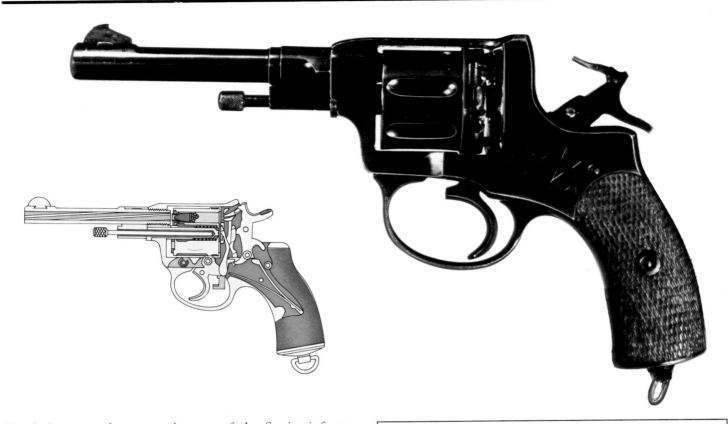

Pistols have not been a main part of the Soviet infantry soldier's weaponry at any time, and in World War II they definitely took a low place on the manufacturing priority. A pistol took about as much time to make as a submachine gun, perhaps more, and the submachine gun was a far better offensive weapon and needed less training to use. So pistol issues do not appear to have changed much from before the war. The probable explanation is that the part of Tula arsenal which was making them before 1941 stayed doing so at the same level, though this has to be speculation since there are no Soviet records to back it up. Tsarist officers carried revolvers, but their Soviet successors preferred a more active part in the battle and do not seem to have complained at carrying the same weapon as their soldiers.

The Soviet revolver was an elderly and complicated design which was all but obsolete in 1940. This was the Nagant, a Belgian product of the late nineteenth century. It originated in Liège from the workshops of Pieper and Nagant. The first supplies for the Tsar's army were made in Belgium, but from about 1901 onwards they were built in the Tula arsenal, which continued to turn them out until 1940, and possibly until 1945. Exactly how many were made is uncertain, though most of the production seems to have been completed in the years between 1902 and 1914.

The Nagant was unusual in that it had a mechanical device to prevent the loss of propellant gas between the face of the cylinder and the breech. On all conventional revolvers there is a small gap between these two parts, and the manufacturer attempts to keep the tolerances tight enough so that the gas

Nagant Model 1895		
Ammunition	7.62mm revol'verni patron obr 1895	
Length	9.06in	229mm
Weight unloaded	1lb 12oz	.79kg
Barrel	4.35in	110mm
Magazine	7-round cylinder	
Muzzle velocity	100ft/sec	305m/sec

leak is minimal and the effect on the bullet too small to be noticed. However, Nagant was not prepared to accept this and arranged for the entire cylinder to be pushed forward as the hammer was cocked. To do this there were special levers and cams in the mechanism, and as the rear face of the cylinder moved away from the support of the standing breech, a resistance plate came up and held the base of the cartridge against the backward force of the propellant. The hammer pin struck through a hole in this plate.

At the front of the cylinder the chamber containing the cartridge was forced onto the barrel, and was coned to fit it better. The cartridge, which was rimmed and carried a 7.62mm bullet, had a case which was longer than the bullet — that is, the case extended beyond the bullet nose and completely enclosed it. This extra length bridged the joint between chamber and barrel and completely sealed it. Thus no gas escaped at all when the round was fired. After firing the cylinder was pushed back by a spring and could then be rotated.

106

It would be pleasing to report that all this complication and expense resulted in a markedly better performance, but regrettably this was not so. There was an increase in muzzle velocity and some reduction in extraneous noise, but little else. It is extraordinary that the Soviets continued to make it for so long and never tried to simplify it.

The other Soviet pistol used during the war was the Tokarev T 33, a fairly straightforward automatic largely based on the Colt Model 1911. Originally brought out in 1930, the military issue was the model 1933, and although this used the same calibre ammunition as the Nagant revolver it was a different round altogether. Before World War I Russia had bought quantities of Mauser pistols, and held stocks of the 7.63mm ammunition which they fired; accordingly the Tokarev design was chambered for a Russian version of this round, with the advantage that the remaining 7.63mm could be used in it. This round, with a rimless cartridge, became the standard pistol and submachine-gun round until the late 1950s. It had virtually the same ballistics as the Mauser, firing a relatively light bullet at fairly high velocity. Although this meant that the energy levels were the same as for larger calibres, the greater velocity made it uncomfortable in a pistol.

Nevertheless, the T 33 was a good weapon. It used the Colt locking system entirely, and the only change was to the locking lugs on the barrel, which were lathe-turned instead of being milled, a change which speeded up production. The hammer mechanism was fitted to a separate assembly in the frame so that it could be removed completely for cleaning, and there was no arrangement for any sort of safety catch beyond a half-cock notch for the hammer.

One very good point was that the feed lips for the ammunition were machined into two arms on the hammer mechanism and so the magazine was flat-topped. This meant that the magazine was far better able to put up with ill-treatment without affecting the feed, for most pistol trouble came from bad feeding caused by damaged magazines.

The Tokarev was first used in action in 1939 in Manchuria and later in that year in Finland. From then on it was generally used on all fronts, mainly by the crews of armoured vehicles and aircraft, and photographs of Soviet pistols being used in action are very few. After the war it was adopted in several of the satellite countries and appeared in Korea in the hands of the Chinese and North Korean troops. It is still the standard pistol of China and several other Communist countries such as Yugoslavia.

Hand-Operated Rifles

The Russian infantry fought the whole of World War II with one of the oldest rifles to be used by any combatant nation. This was the Moissin Nagant, a design dating from 1891 and owing at least part of its working to the Belgian firm of Nagant, who had produced the gas-seal revolver. Nagant designed a clip-loading five-shot magazine and feed system

---

Pistolet Obr 1933 (T 33)

Ammunition	7.62mm patron obr 1930g	
Length	7.68in	193mm
Weight unloaded	1lb 13oz	.83kg
Barrel	4.57in	116mm
Magazine	8-round detachable box	
Muzzle velocity	1375ft/sec	418m/sec

which was allied to a bolt-action rifle which appeared under the direction of a Colonel Moissin. The resulting weapon was robust, straightforward to make, relatively simple and extremely serviceable. The only criticism that has ever been levelled at it is that the bolt, which was made in two parts, was needlessly complicated, but it probably had to be in order to avoid patent rights in the many designs current at that time.

The Moissin Nagant was made in huge numbers for the Tsarist army, mainly in Russia in the Tula, Sestroryetsk and Ishevsk arsenals, but also in Belgium, France and Switzerland, where contracts were laid while the arsenals in Russia were tooling up. Manufacture continued until at least 1945, although the rifle was out of date long before then.

The original 1891 model was replaced by later versions, the main one being the 1930 variant. Up to 1930 the calibre was known as 'three line', a line being one tenth of an inch, or 2.54mm, and the range was calibrated on the backsight in arshins, which were about 0.72m. The Russian Revolution swept away these mediaeval relics, the calibre became 7.62mm and new backsights were fitted with the range in metres. None of these alterations made any difference to the ammunition, which was still the 1908-pattern rimmed round, much similar in appearance and performance to the British .303in or the US 30-06 Winchester.

By 1940 there were one or two other variants in service also. The main issue was the rifle, Type 1891/30, which was the standard weapon of the infantry. This was a long weapon, 51in (1.3m), weighing the usual rifle weight of 9lb 10oz (3.98kg). The five-shot magazine was an obvious disadvantage in modern times and it had one peculiarity forced upon it by the ammunition it used. There was a small catch in the magazine which held down the second round in the column, allowing the top one to be fed without undue pressure under it. This made it easier for the bolt to pick it up and slide it forward. Without the catch the top round jammed its rim frequently. No other nation found it necessary to go to these lengths to get good feeding, but the 1908-pattern round does have a most distinctive rim, which affected other weapons also. The holding-down catch was released as the bolt came forward, and it then allowed the next round to be pushed upwards.

The long rifle was clumsy and awkward to carry, and it was supplemented by a shorter carbine version derived from one specifically produced for dragoons in 1910. This carbine was modernized in 1930 and again in 1938, both versions being all but identical and only differing from the long rifle in that they had shorter barrels. The 1938 carbine did not carry a bayonet, but strangely enough one was demanded during the war. Once more the design was amended, and the model of 1944 was given a folding bayonet permanently attached to the muzzle and folding to the right side for stowage. This was apparently popular and was copied in several of the satellite countries, though not until the war was over.

A feature of the Moissin Nagants was in all cases their bayonet. From the first models this was a long thin spike of cruciform shape, much like the ones the early muskets carried. To make matters worse the Russian Army did not issue scabbards and the soldiers carried their bayonets fixed at all times. This practice was well on its way out by the time of World War II, but it helps to explain the mentality which led to the folding version.

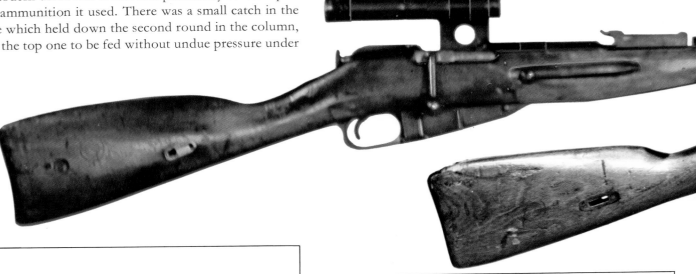

Moissin Nagant M1891/30

Ammunition	7.62mm patron obr 91g	
Length	48.5in	1232mm
Weight unloaded	8lb 11oz	3.95kg
Barrel	28.7in	728mm
Magazine	5-round integral box	
Muzzle velocity	2800ft/sec	853m/sec

Nagant Carbine M91/30

Ammunition	7.62mm patron obr 91g	
Length	40.1in	1019mm
Weight unloaded	7lb 11oz	3.4kg
Barrel	20in	508mm
Magazine	5-round integral box	
Muzzle velocity	2655ft/sec	808m/sec

A significant number of long rifles were used for sniping, and the Soviets made much fuss over their snipers, particularly their women snipers, who were useful for propaganda photographs. The sniping rifles were fitted with a PU telescopic sight of 3.5 power magnification. This was an awkward sight to use, as it was short and the firer's head was in the wrong position. It was later supplemented by the PE of 4 power, which was both longer and nearer the eye position. Both types fitted into a dovetail mounting block on the left of the body, and these mounting blocks were the external indications of the sniping versions. The only other

Below: Troops move forward on the Leningrad front with the Moissin Nagant's extremely long bayonet fixed.

indication of the sniping use was that the bolt handle was turned down to clear the telescope. Presumably the rifles themselves were specially selected and gauged, since the normal issue was fairly rough and ready.

Manufacture ceased entirely in Russia in 1945, but by that time there were several millions of the Moissin Nagants in existence. They continued in Soviet service until the early 1950s when the new self-loading series replaced them at last, after 60 years of continuous use. The satellite countries used them for much longer, and both the long and carbine versions were carried by the North Koreans and Chinese in Korea. In these and other countries they were used until the ubiquitous Kalashnikov took over throughout the Communist zone in the late 1950s.

Self-Loading Rifles

Although the Soviet Army spent a great deal of money in 1930 and 1932 modernizing its elderly Moissin Nagants, there was a lively appreciation of the fact that for modern warfare the only sensible infantry weapon was a self-loading rifle with a reasonable magazine capacity, and some studies were put in hand. These resulted in 1936 in the limited issue of the Model 1936 Simonov rifle, known as the AVS 36, an abbreviation of Automaticheskia Vintovka Simonova Obrazets 1936G.

The Simonov suffered from two defects, complexity and limited strength. These were sufficient to defeat it within a year or two of use by the troops. The complexity arose because Simonov had chosen a rather complicated method of

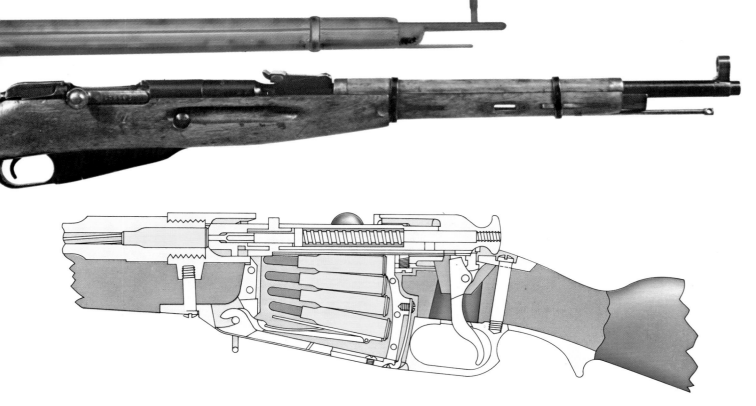

locking by using a vertical locking block which was cammed up into recesses in the bolt as the bolt closed. This block then firmly held the bolt against the breech until the usual gas action took place and the piston rod shoved the bolt carrier backwards, whereupon it cammed the locking piece downwards and pushed the bolt rearwards. Unfortunately Simonov chose to make his system in fairly small, delicate pieces all requiring careful machining and fitting to work properly, yet at the same time being susceptible to wear. Matters were made worse by the fact that as the bolt moved backwards and forwards in the body, it was exposed to the air, allowing dirt and grit to get in and be mixed with the lubricating oil. From then on wear of the moving parts was inevitable.

The second general defect was a lack of strength in the mechanism. The components were not capable of standing up to field use without breaking because so much effort had been put into weight saving. Another difficulty was an uncomfortable muzzle blast and recoil, which a prominent and rather ugly cylindrical muzzle brake apparently did not entirely overcome. On the other hand, Simonov correctly

Simonov and had the same type of perforated sheet steel for the fore hand-guard, though there were minor differences in the actual manufacture.

The Tokarev designs were more workmanlike than the Simonov, though even so they were not entirely successful in wartime. They were gas-operated, with a variable gas port and a long-stroke piston working on a bolt carrier which slid to and fro in a heavy, machined body. The muzzle of the rifle had an unusual sleeve screwed onto it and this sleeve carried the foresight, muzzle-brake, and gas port, the idea being to reduce the amount of machining needed on the barrel itself and allow it to be made on existing machinery set up for the bolt-action rifles. The locking system was again unusual but simple. The bolt locked by tilting downwards, its rear surface being crammed into a recess in the bottom of the body. The action is much like that of a Bren gun upside down. To allow for changes in cartridge head space – a failing on the Simonov – the locking shoulder in the body could be taken out and other sizes fitted.

The general construction required a good deal of careful machining and fitting, but there were better arrangements

appreciated the need for a sensible magazine size and he fitted one to carry 15 rounds, together with an adjustable gas regulator and a cleaning rod beneath the barrel. Finally it had a change lever to allow automatic fire, a method of firing which allegedly shook it to pieces.

By 1938 the Simonov was out of favour and being replaced with the first of a series of Tokarev designs known as SVT for Samozariadnyia Vintovka Tokareva, or Self-Loading Tokarev. These were very similar in general outline to the

SVT 40		
Ammunition	7.62mm patron obr 91g	
Length	48.27in	1226mm
Weight unloaded	8lb 9oz	3.9kg
Barrel	24.2in	610mm
Magazine	10-round detachable box	
Muzzle velocity	2756ft/sec	840m/sec

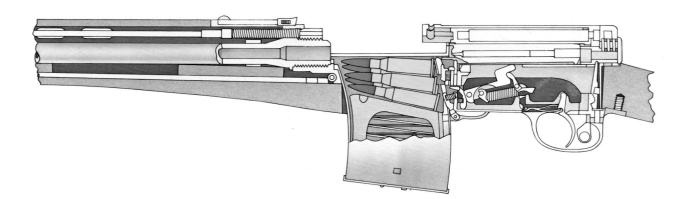

for taking up wear, and the action had a permanent dust cover to keep it clean. The 1938 design showed itself to be sound enough, but a little frail in action, and it was replaced with the 1940 pattern, which lasted throughout the war. One improvement over the 1938 pattern was the use of a one-piece wooden stock, as the two-piece one on the '38 had shown itself too ready to split. In 1942 an automatic version, the AVT, was introduced, but apparently this was not a complete success since the mechanism could not stand automatic fire for long.

The main failing of the Tokarevs was that they were frail. Too much weight was shaved off in order to keep them within acceptable limits for an infantryman to carry in action, and the result was a rifle that had to be carefully looked after on the battlefield. The Russian soldier was not renowned for caring for his equipment, and the Tokarevs were mostly issued to NCOs or selected soldiers. They found extensive use as sniping rifles, using selected barrels, since the semi-automatic action allowed the sniper the chance of a rapid second shot without having to disturb his aim. He could also be expected to look after his rifle and apply a little intelligence in handling it.

The sniping versions carried the usual PU and PE telescopes mounted on special brackets screwed to the left side of the body, where they were more rigidly fixed than on the Moissin Nagants, and also easier to use. It is interesting that the Germans used their semi-automatic rifles for sniping also, probably for the same reasons as did the Soviets. One wonders who thought of it first, for the German Gewehr 41s and 43s were extensively issued for the Eastern Front.

The Tokarevs were not made after 1944, one difficulty being that the machine tools required for them were only held in one or two arsenals, and so the manufacture could not be spread around. However, the Soviets apparently did not regard it as a failure since it continued in service after the war until replaced by the later models of self-loading rifles in the late 1940s. It had a fair span of service life, having been first used in Finland in 1940, and its difficulties may have arisen more from the ammunition it had to fire than from any fault in its design and manufacture. Perhaps one should not be too hard on the Simonovs and Tokarevs; they may have had many troubles not of their own making.

Submachine Guns

The Soviets took up the idea of submachine guns rather sooner than the other countries in Europe, and produced a 1934 design by Degtyarev which was tried out in the Spanish Civil War from about 1937 onwards. The Degtyarev was not a particularly inspired weapon; in fact it was very much based on the German MP 28, which seems to have been a general pattern for several nationalities to copy. The difference in the Degtyarev lay in its feed, which was from a drum, although the drum ended in a short column which was actually the part that went into the housing. This peculiar arrangement was retained through several modifications until 1940, when a more straightforward weapon came out in which manufacture had been much simplified and the Finnish Suomi drum had been taken almost in its entirety.

The 1940 pattern was a better proposition in several ways, in particular the internal lining of the barrel, which was chromed. This refinement is only rarely found in other weapons, but the Soviets used it a good deal, and the PPD 1940 was the first to incorporate it as standard. It made the barrel last much longer by resisting wear and rust, and needed less intense cleaning by the gunner. In other words, it survived neglect.

The calibre of this and all the subsequent Soviet guns was 7.62mm Soviet Pistol, a rather elderly cartridge derived from the Mauser 7.63mm and having the unusual feature of being bottle-necked. No other nation tried to use bottle-necked cartridges in submachine guns, but the Soviets were forced to by the exigencies of existing ammunition production, and in fact it worked well. The calibre was smaller than was usually used, so that the bullet was lighter, but the muzzle velocity was higher, and at the ranges that submachine guns were used the difference was scarcely noticeable.

The PPD 40 was never produced in large quantities, and it seems that few were used in action. In 1941, when the results of the Winter War had been absorbed, it was decided that submachine guns were to become a major fighting weapon, and would be needed in large numbers. The PPD 40 was not well suited to manufacture in these quantities and so a new design was called for. This was undertaken by Georg Shpagin and he retained the Suomi drum and the 7.62mm cartridge, but in all other respects aimed for mass production with no frills. The result was the unbelievably successful PPSh-41, a weapon which despite its crudities and agricultural appearance was still in many ways a more refined proposition than the Sten. In the PPSh the Soviets used steel pressings and welding for the first time, and in order to save complication the simple blowback design could only fire automatic and had a very basic safety system. The stock was wooden, but Russia has plenty of wood, and for the first production, when the German invasion was at its height, the barrels were made by cutting up old 7.62mm rifle barrels and making two submachine-gun barrels from one rifle. Luckily the twist of the rifling was roughly the same.

The number of parts was kept to the inescapable minimum, and was little more than the bolt, its spring and extractor, and three or four pressed parts in the trigger group. The magazine line had been set up for the PPD, and so it continued to make the same drum throughout the war, as this was probably the most difficult part of the entire weapon. The various state arsenals and commandeered factories

turned out enormous numbers of the PPSh between 1941 and 1945, the total being somewhere near five million. Reliability was good, mainly because there was nothing that could go wrong, and the gun itself was able to stand up to the most appalling ill-treatment without suffering at all. The magazine was the weakest part, and there were plenty of spares.

When the Soviet Army found itself able to strike back in 1942 and 1943 there were never enough infantry weapons to equip all the troops, and the deficit was largely made up with PPSh submachine guns. Whole units were armed with nothing else, including huge numbers of partisans behind the German lines. The whole philosophy of the Soviet tactics was in any case based on the idea of attacking all the time, and a submachine gun is ideal for this sort of war. It is not a weapon that one can use for sniping or harassing fire; it is essentially meant for dynamic close-quarter fighting, and that was how it was used. By disregarding casualties altogether the Soviet infantry was able to swamp the German defences and pour in a storm of fire from close range that nothing could withstand. In the town fighting in places like Stalingrad and Leningrad the submachine gun was supreme, and it was after Stalingrad that the Germans tried to give their guns a double magazine to keep pace with the 71-round drum on the PPSh. In fact the Germans used the PPSh themselves, boring out captured ones to 9mm and fitting their own magazines, though the result was not an unqualified success.

Although the PPSh-41 was the standard submachine gun throughout the war, and indeed for long after also, so that it became a symbol of Communism itself, it was not the only one in service. Apart from the PPD-40, which as we have seen was never used in great numbers, there were two more, the PPS-42 and 43. Pundits differ as to whether there really was a PPS-42, or whether it is just the early version of the

Pistolet Pulemyot Shpagina obr 1941G (PPSh-41)		
Ammunition	7.62mm pistoletnyi patron obr 1930g	
Length	33in	838mm
Weight unloaded	8lb	3.64kg
Barrel	10.5in	266mm
Magazine	35-round detachable box or	
	71-round drum	
Cyclic rate	900rpm	
Muzzle velocity	1600ft/sec	488m/sec

PPS-43, but it is not important. The 43 undoubtedly existed, and may still do so. Whether its first models were known by another name, or whether they have subsequently been given that name, does not matter too greatly, since the differences are slight. (The Soviet Army is not given to helping foreign weapon students to classify its weapons.)

Left: A posed photograph of defenders of Stalingrad, 1944. Two men carry PPSh-41 machine guns, while the third is armed with a DP-28 light machine gun.

Right: Factory workers armed with PPSh-41s. The clumsy drum is well evident; unlike the American Thompson, this weapon retained its drum magazine throughout the war.

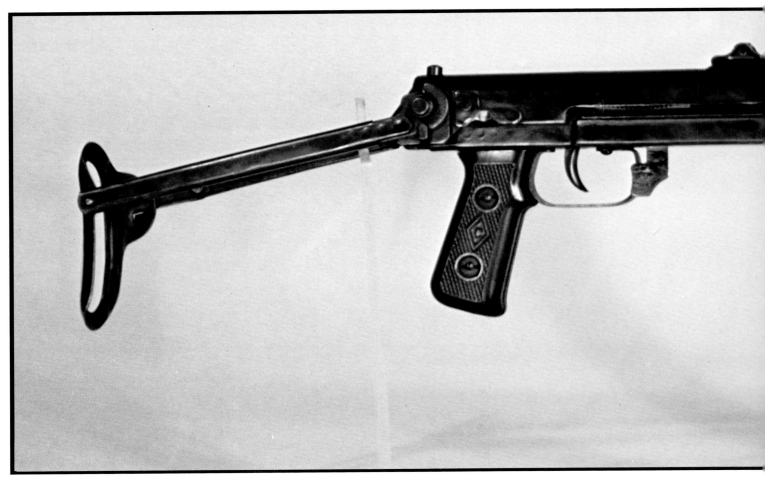

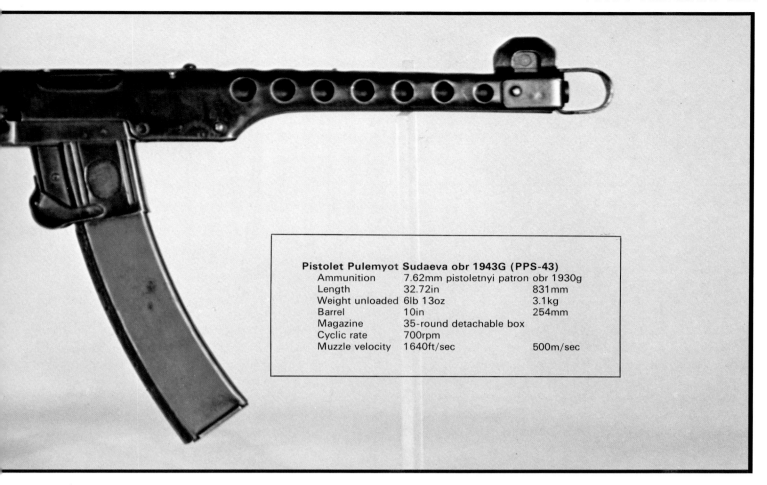

Pistolet Pulemyot Sudaeva obr 1943G (PPS-43)

Ammunition	7.62mm pistoletnyi patron obr 1930g	
Length	32.72in	831mm
Weight unloaded	6lb 13oz	3.1kg
Barrel	10in	254mm
Magazine	35-round detachable box	
Cyclic rate	700rpm	
Muzzle velocity	1640ft/sec	500m/sec

Left: Soldiers armed with PPS-43s give covering fire for their comrades during the fighting in Budapest.

The PPS-43 was designed by Sudarev, perhaps as a replacement for the 41, or perhaps simply as a back-up design in case of need. The need came during the siege of Leningrad, when most supplies to the city were almost cut off and weapons were short. The 43 was made in the city factories in large numbers and delivered straight to the troops in the line, the first field trials being done in action. Luckily it succeeded from the beginning, and became a vital factor in arming the troops defending the city. When the siege was raised in 1942 the factories continued to build it and it was issued to the Soviet Army in general, though not in particularly large numbers, and production apparently ceased before 1945. After the war it was given to the satellite countries, some of whom built it, or adaptations of it, for years, and it can still be found in some corners of Asia.

In fact, the PPS-43 deserved a better fate, for it was a practical design and must have been every bit as good as the PPSh-41. It was built almost entirely of mild steel, stamped, pressed and welded, with as few components as possible. The only non-metal parts were the pistol grip, which was plastic, and a leather buffer behind the bolt. The barrel and bolt were the only machined components; the sights were crude and the finish rough. It used a 35-round box magazine which was peculiar to it, though it was later adapted for the PPSh-41 and may be seen in a very few photographs on the latter. Like the 41 the barrel jacket ran forward beyond the muzzle to make a simple compensator to reduce muzzle climb, and like the 41 again it only fired on automatic. It is now most difficult to decide how many of these guns were actually made. It must have been at least half a million, though perhaps not much more, at least not in Russia.

Machine Guns

When the new Red Army began re-equipping itself in the early 1920s, one weapon which it badly needed was a light machine gun for the infantry. An attempt was made to capitalize on the existing tooling and machinery for making the Maxim, and a light Maxim was tried, but it was no more successful than the German models of 1915 and 1918, and it was obvious that there would have to be a completely new design. In the end it was produced by Vasily Degtyarev, one of the great names in Soviet weapon history. He submitted his model for testing in 1926, and it was adopted as the model of 1927, sometimes quoted as 1928. In Russian the name for it was Pulemet Degtyareva Pekhotnii, normally abbreviated to DP.

The DP was a triumph of simplicity, for it only had six moving parts in the operating system with a consequent gain in reliability and strength over many other ideas which were

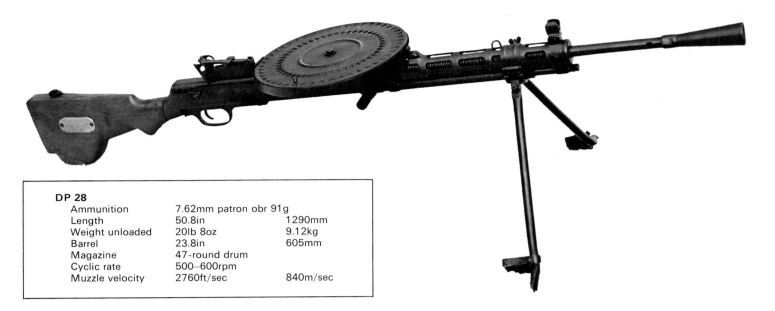

DP 28		
Ammunition	7.62mm patron obr 91g	
Length	50.8in	1290mm
Weight unloaded	20lb 8oz	9.12kg
Barrel	23.8in	605mm
Magazine	47-round drum	
Cyclic rate	500–600rpm	
Muzzle velocity	2760ft/sec	840m/sec

current at that time. The system worked by gas, using the long-stroke principle, but with a few innovations which were specifically put in to ease the problem of manufacture. It was of course made to the methods of its day, namely by machining solid forgings to reasonably fine tolerances, but Degtyarev went to a lot of trouble to reduce all the unnecessary work and the gun was probably one of the cheapest and easiest machine guns to make of any nation in the war.

There were two specific peculiarities. One was the locking system; this used a pair of flaps either side of the bolt, which were pushed outwards by a large-diameter firing pin as it went forward to strike the cartridge. The flaps were hinged at the front, and the pin opened them out at the back, where

Below: Covering an advance with a DP-28 machine gun. This particular one does not have the usual muzzle flash-hider.

they locked into recesses cut in the sides of the body. The result was a perfectly safe and positive lock, for the cartridge could not be fired until the bolt was held by both flaps, and the bolt could not be unlocked until the gas piston had retracted the firing pin. This useful idea was first invented in Sweden in the late nineteenth century, but it had never been used other than for experiments before Degtyarev took it up.

The other speciality of the DP was the magazine. Degtyarev wanted a magazine rather than a belt in order to save weight, but the rimmed 1891/1908 round was, and still is, very liable to jam when fed from a box magazine in a straight column. So he put the rounds in a circular pan and pushed them downwards out of a slot by rotating the top of the pan with a spring. The result was an entirely reliable and trouble-free magazine holding no less than 47 rounds, at a time when most light machine guns were using 30-round boxes. However, the round pan was not all that easy to carry and it could be damaged by rough handling; also it was fiddly and slow to load. To carry the ammunition the number two of the gun team had a steel case containing three full magazines, which must have been a heavy enough load for even a Russian soldier.

This remarkable gun was issued on a scale of one to each infantry section of ten men and fought throughout the war without any significant change. In fact, it had some active service before that in Manchuria, Spain and Finland, and it says a good deal for Degtyarev's foresight that these widely different conditions brought about no alterations to the design. In late 1944 it was realized that the recoil spring, which was beneath the barrel, became weak with prolonged use due to the heat from the barrel altering the tempering, and it was moved to the rear of the body and housed in an ugly projection above the butt. This prolonged its life, but made the gun slightly less pleasant to handle, and a pistol grip was fitted for the gunner's right hand.

The success of the DP caused it to be adapted for vehicle and aircraft use. The tank gun was simply the DP with the butt removed and a pistol grip substituted, and a larger magazine holding 60 rounds. After the first models were tried a heavier barrel was fitted to cope with the greater rate of fire. The aircraft gun was similar to the tank version, and was a rather desperate expedient since the rate of fire was far too low for air fighting.

The infantry guns allowed the gunner to change the barrel relatively easily, though not as well as the Czech ZB series, since there was no carrying handle to lift off the hot parts. The DP series only fired automatic, the bolt remaining at the rear after each burst, and the only safety was a grip behind the trigger guard which had to be squeezed to release the trigger for firing. A simple bipod, a wooden butt and open sights ranging up to 1,500m completed the minor equipment on the gun. It lasted in service until the arrival of the RP-46 after the

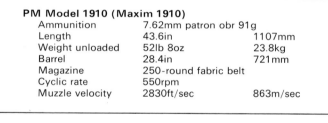

PM Model 1910 (Maxim 1910)		
Ammunition	7.62mm patron obr 91g	
Length	43.6in	1107mm
Weight unloaded	52lb 8oz	23.8kg
Barrel	28.4in	721mm
Magazine	250-round fabric belt	
Cyclic rate	550rpm	
Muzzle velocity	2830ft/sec	863m/sec

war. There is no record of the number made, but it must have been enormous.

For a support machine gun the Soviets used a version of the Maxim, which they had had in service since 1905. The World War II guns were the model of 1910, and the arsenals were well tooled-up to produce it. There were in any case large numbers in stock in 1941, and this was just as well since it takes time to make a Maxim, and it needs skilled men. The advantage of the Maxim was that it was reliable and could use rimmed ammunition without jamming, just the same reasons that persuaded the British to stick to the Vickers. The same drawbacks were there as well – bulk, water-cooling, great complexity in manufacture, and weight. From the beginning in 1905, when they first built Maxims, the Russians managed to make the heaviest of any nation. In World War II the Model 1910 weighed 52lb 8oz (23.8kg), but with it came the mounting, which added another 110lb (50kg), and even the toughest Russian peasant must have blenched when faced with that lot. To ease the burden the gun was given little wheels and the crew towed it behind them, like a miniature artillery piece without a limber. This was the 'Sokolov' mount, with a U-shaped steel tube as a trail behind and two legs which swing forward for extra stability when firing, but these legs were abandoned later to simplify production. Some of the early models had a small steel shield to protect the gunner, but this added another 56lb (25.5kg), and it too went soon enough.

In winter the Sokolovs were given small skis, and there were also a small issue of ordinary tripods instead of Sokolovs, but these seem to have been unpopular and few appear in photographs. The difficulties of operating a Maxim, particularly in winter when the cooling water would have to be

Above: A captured Maxim 1910 machine gun with its Sokolov mounting.

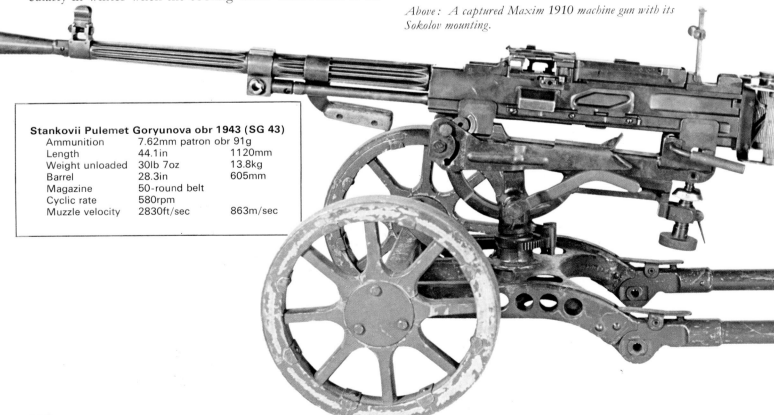

Stankovii Pulemet Goryunova obr 1943 (SG 43)		
Ammunition	7.62mm patron obr 91g	
Length	44.1in	1120mm
Weight unloaded	30lb 7oz	13.8kg
Barrel	28.3in	605mm
Magazine	50-round belt	
Cyclic rate	580rpm	
Muzzle velocity	2830ft/sec	863m/sec

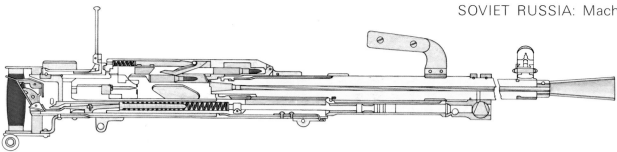

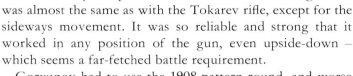

kept from freezing, must have been appalling, but as with all the Maxim family the reward was reliability and long life. The Maxim survived the war to continue into the Korean conflict with no alterations, though it passed out of Soviet service in 1946. China held on to her Maxims until at least 1962, and perhaps later. It still appears in some of the smaller countries, and has been met on a few occasions in the Arabian peninsula until quite recently.

By 1941 the Maxim had been in use in the Soviet Army for nearly four decades and its replacement became a matter of urgency. Despite its virtues, the factory effort needed to make it was far more than the country could stand, and the nation's designers were driven hard to find a modern gun. Degtyarev, the great favourite and probably the most prolific designer of small arms since John Browning, did his best, but he ended up with one of his rare failures. He produced an enlarged version of his DP, using the same system of locking and gas operation, with a long finned barrel, a heavy square body, and the ability to be carried on the same mountings as the Maxim. Feed was by belt, either the Maxim canvas belt or a metal-link one. The performance of the Degtyarev was all that was wanted, but it was too difficult to make in quantity, and only a few were issued. The Soviet Army looked for other ideas.

The one that they chose was the Goryunov, or Stankovii Pulemet Goryunova Obrazets 1943, known as the SG43. Peter Maximovitch Goryunov produced a workable design of sustained-fire gun in 1942. There are suspicions nowadays that Goryunov had been working on a tank machine gun for some time beforehand, since his gun had features that were not usual in infantry guns – the weight of the barrel, for instance. But whatever the background, the gun worked and was accepted.

Goryunov chose to use long-stroke gas operation and locked the breech block by tilting it, but he tilted it to one side – a most unusual arrangement since it was usually thought that in doing this an unbalanced strain was put on one side of the body, with consequent possibilities of inaccuracy in shooting. However, Goryunov made the body thick enough to look after this sort of loading, and there

were never any complaints on that score. The locking action was almost the same as with the Tokarev rifle, except for the sideways movement. It was so reliable and strong that it worked in any position of the gun, even upside-down – which seems a far-fetched battle requirement.

Goryunov had to use the 1908-pattern round, and worse still, the Maxim cloth belts. With the cloth belt each round had to be pulled out backwards, because of the rim on the case. Goryunov not only arranged for that to be done, but he also designed a metal-link belt – an improvement on the cloth, which took up water and swelled, jamming the gun. His 50-round metal belts could be joined together to give a belt of any desired length, or carried on the gun ready to fire for the price of little extra weight.

Unlike the Maxim the Goryunov barrel was air-cooled, and could be changed quite quickly by a trained crew. Unlike the Maxim, again, the Goryunov was fairly easy to make, as it had far fewer parts. The designer boasted that the only spring necessary to work the gun was the return spring, housed in a telescoping guide. Great attention was also paid to arranging for the gunner to get at the feed mechanism to clear stoppages, a reflection perhaps of the poor ammunition production in Russia. The gun dismantled easily without special tools.

Many of the Goryunovs were mounted on the Sokolov mounting, but the trend changed towards the end of the war and a standard tripod evolved in 1930 was more often used. For one thing, it was easier to make and used less metal.

The Goryunov never replaced the Maxim as the company support machine gun because not enough of them could be made. But as soon as the war finished it was officially brought in as the next generation of support gun throughout the army, even being fitted to tanks, and so it remains to this day, having been used by all the satellites also. It has been manufactured all over the Eastern bloc, and though there have been, and still are, variants of one sort or another, in general it survives in the form in which it first appeared 35 years ago.

Anti-Tank Rifles

As early as 1930 Soviet Russia saw as clearly as any other nation that some sort of anti-tank weapon was going to be needed for the infantry in future wars, and in 1932 an attempt was made to produce a recoilless rifle in 37mm. It was a bold step but it failed, and the requirement was changed to that of a standard large-bore conventional rifle, just the same as everyone else was making. There was little success with any of the types tried. One report speaks of no less than 15 different models being tried between 1936 and 1938, none of which met the requirement.

In the end the Soviet Army ordered that the World War I Mauser was to be copied, but Sokolov, who was undertaking the modification, decided to use the existing Soviet 12.7mm heavy-machine-gun cartridge rather than manufacture the special Mauser round. At the same time he introduced a five-round magazine. The rifle was perfectly practical, simple to make and reasonably portable; the difficulty was that the round lacked sufficient power and could not penetrate even 12mm of armour at 400m. Some of these inadequate weapons were used in the Winter War against Finland in 1939/40, and presumably reinforced the findings of the official tests. In any case the Soviet Army tried again in 1939 and this time at least three designs were submitted, each using the then new 14.5mm round which was from another heavy machine gun.

The 1939 series were not much better – the one produced by Shpitalny apparently having a flame-thrower in it, and Vladimirov's requiring two men to operate it. Rukavshinkov designed a semi-automatic rifle which showed promise and was followed up for the next two years, though without much success. By that time the Soviet Army, in near despair, was considering copying the German PzB 39. However, before committing themselves to the German model they had one more try at getting a home-produced rifle. Two experienced designers, Degtyarev and Simonov, were given the task, and bidden to use the 14.5mm round.

Simonov elected to go for a semi-automatic system and in due course produced the PTRS 41 (Protivotankovyi Ruzhe Simonova Obrazets 1941 G, to give it its full title). This was an enormously long – 84in (2m) – and heavy – 46lb (21kg) – weapon, and to help in carrying it the barrel dismounted from the body by a simple wedge-bolt. The system of operation was the classical long-stroke gas piston, and the bolt locked by forward lugs in the barrel extension. Ammunition was fed from a magazine below the body, and to load this magazine it was swung downwards and a clip pushed into it. The magazine was then shut against the body and it pushed the top round into the way of the bolt. From then on the gunner simply had to pull the trigger for each shot.

The gas supply of the PTRS could be altered to take account of dirt or frost, and theoretically it was an ideal weapon. Unfortunately it was made rather too light and tended to be unreliable and prone to breakages, but it was made in large quantities and issued throughout the army for the whole period of the war. After 1945 it virtually disappeared. Although there have been various reports of its use from time to time since, it has usually transpired that these have been confusions with the PTRD, its sister gun.

The PTRD was designed by Degtyarev at the same time and followed a different trend of thought. Degtyarev aimed for the simplest possible weapon for the purposes of manufacture and reliability. He produced a single-shot bolt-action

Right: The spoils of war – a German soldier examines a stack of captured PTRD anti-tank rifles. These rifles proved extremely effective against light tanks.

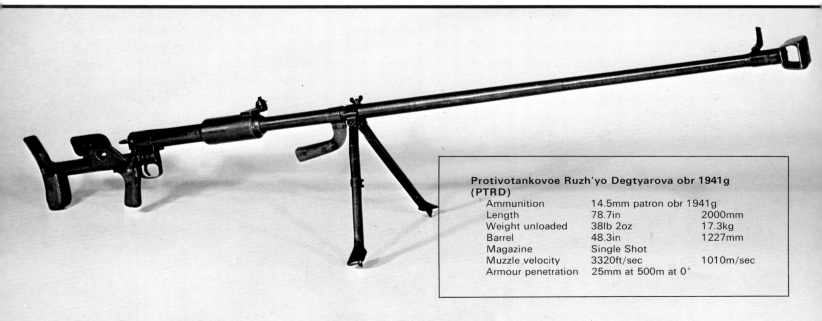

Protivotankovoe Ruzh'yo Degtyarova obr 1941g (PTRD)		
Ammunition	14.5mm patron obr 1941g	
Length	78.7in	2000mm
Weight unloaded	38lb 2oz	17.3kg
Barrel	48.3in	1227mm
Magazine	Single Shot	
Muzzle velocity	3320ft/sec	1010m/sec
Armour penetration	25mm at 500m at 0°	

rifle which, though straightforward, was remarkably ingenious in its conception. Like the PTRS it was long, but this was a function of using the 14.5mm cartridge; however, it was lighter, turning the scales at 38lb (17.5kg). It did not disassemble for carriage, so it was probably a more difficult weapon to carry than the PTRS; on the other hand it had an enviable reputation for reliability.

The design was simplicity itself. The barrel ended in a tubular body which was almost an extension of the barrel,

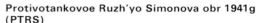

Protivotankovoe Ruzh'yo Simonova obr 1941g (PTRS)		
Ammunition	14.5mm patron obr 1941g	
Length	86.61in	2134mm
Weight unloaded	46lb 3oz	20.86kg
Barrel	48in	1220mm
Magazine	5-round clip-loaded box	
Muzzle velocity	3320ft/sec	1010m/sec
Armour penetration	25mm at 500m at 0°	

and the bolt worked in this. The butt and pistol grip were on a slide, and the barrel and body recoiled along this slide, thereby absorbing some of the recoil and making it a less unpleasant rifle to fire than the Simonov. As the bolt recoiled, it rode up a shaped plate on the side of the slide, and was automatically opened. It was then held back while the barrel ran forward again, extracting the empty case at the same time. All the gunner had to do was to drop another cartridge into the breech and close the bolt. Although the author has never had the opportunity to fire this particular weapon and form his own judgement, it must have been capable of quite rapid fire, certainly fast enough for anti-tank work.

These rifles were issued on the scale of one to each platoon from the end of 1941 onwards, and though they can have been of little value in stopping the German Mark IIIs and IVs, they would have been effective enough against the lighter vehicles and were also used frequently to engage machine guns and defensive positions. They were easily hidden and easily moved, and with their powerful round the effective range against light targets was really only limited by how far the gunner could see. Later on, some were used in Korea as sniping rifles. There are accounts of UN positions coming under harassing sniper fire at ranges up to 1,500m, and being able to do nothing in retaliation.

The PTRD must have been a better proposition than the Simonov since it was taken into service in several of the Eastern-bloc armies after the war ended. In the late 1960s it was still to be found in the Albanian Army, and one was captured a couple of years ago from some Dhofari rebels in Oman.

THE UNITED STATES

The United States has always had a strong civilian arms industry and guns have traditionally played a part in the upbringing of every American boy. Not that boys who play with guns necessarily make better soldiers – but it does mean that there is an appreciation of the use of weapons and the care of them, the latter often being more important in war-time. The strong home industry was the corner-stone of the US method of procurement of small arms, and indeed it still is. It meant that in peace-time the small quantities of weapons and ammunition needed by the regular army could be easily met from the output from the government arsenals, in particular Springfield. When the demand rose above the capacity of these establishments, contracts were laid out to industry, which could start producing with minimum delay. It was a system which was used to good effect in both world wars.

Firms such as Colt, Winchester, Remington, Smith & Wesson, Harrington and Richardson, and many, many others were only too ready to pick up government contracts, though the competition was usually severe, and sometimes the US Government was by no means generous with its prices. But these firms could, and did, turn the United States into the arsenal of the Free World during the critical years of World War II.

The weapons that they made were selected by the Ordnance Department of the Department of the Army. They usually gave the actual job of selection of specific weapons to a board constituted for that one task, so there are frequent references to the Board of Ordnance, or the Ordnance Board – all very confusing because the British have an Ordnance Board, too, but it does a different job. Anyway, the American method of selecting weapon designs was little different from that of any other country, but when ideas went out to industry the response was usually far greater. For instance, when the tender for a light carbine was offered to the US arms industry in 1941, no less than 25 separate and distinct designs were offered for trial. All of them were tried, too, creating great difficulty for the Aberdeen Proving Ground, which had to show that all had been given a fair test.

But the omnipotence of the Department of the Army was apparently challenged from time to time, and with success. In July 1945 the president of the Pacific War Board requested 15,000 short M1 rifles. To speed things up he ordered the ordnance unit under his command to make up 150 as a trial lot, and sent one to Washington to show them what he was talking about in case his meaning had been distorted in transmission. Washington obliged by putting out an order for 15,000, but the war ended before any work was done. At this distance in time it is difficult to judge the precise grada-tions of power between the various boards, but it does seem from this example that there was more than one voice in the small-arms world in the US forces. Perhaps there were

several equal voices, since the request of the Pacific War Board was apparently never questioned.

The overall policy for the selection and manufacture of infantry small arms in the US forces cannot be faulted. Unlike the Germans, Italians and Japanese, the Americans stuck rigidly to certain calibres of ammunition and certain designs of weapon. As we have seen, in war-time this has definite advantages, provided that the right choice was made in the beginning. In the US the right choice was most certainly made. The 30–06 cartridge, while open to a good deal of criticism today, had few equals in 1940 despite its age. The .45in ACP pistol cartridge might not have been everyone's selection for close-quarter fighting, but it gave a knock-down blow (or so the Americans believed) and it was available in large quantities. The choice of a self-loading rifle in the difficult days of the Depression was a master stroke, and the determination to push it through the many committees who must have tried to kill it could only have been provided by a man like Douglas MacArthur. The Browning series of machine guns were also the right ones for the job, though one has to be charitable about the BAR. The great thing about the American weaponry was that though the Department of the Army was surrounded by inventors and manufacturers who were boiling over with ideas, all being pushed with typical American energy, yet the Department held their line and stuck to a small number of known and proven designs which they could rely on. It must have taken nerve at times, but it paid off handsomely.

Below: US Marines wade ashore at Tinian, keeping their M1 carbines and Garand M1 rifles clear of the water.

The troops who used these weapons were organized into infantry battalions looking much like any other country's, with one minor exception. This was the weapons platoon in each rifle company, and the weapons company in each battalion. Whereas practically all other battalions in the war had some sort of support company, the US Army went one better with a weapons platoon in the company as well. This platoon carried some mortars and some machine guns, and it gave the company commander a little extra firepower to play with on his own. As a result, the US infantry company was a more formidable force than any other, and was well able to take care of itself provided that it had the ammunition that it needed. It had always been an axiom of the US Army that fire-power counts more than anything else, and the volume of fire that an American infantry company could put down was quite remarkable.

There were some interesting gaps in the American armoury. For instance, there was never a satisfactory grenade launcher, though some were issued. Grenades were hand-thrown in the US Army, and it may have been that the lavish mortar and artillery support made rifle-launched grenades unnecessary. Another was the lack of a squad light machine gun, which is referred to in detail in the section on machine guns. There were other gaps, but they are outside the particular area of small arms. However, no matter what the shortcomings might have been, in general the US soldier was well armed, well supplied and extremely well supported. He went to war with a strong and comprehensive system behind him, using robust and reliable weapons supplied with plenty of ammunition. It was a winning combination, and it won convincingly.

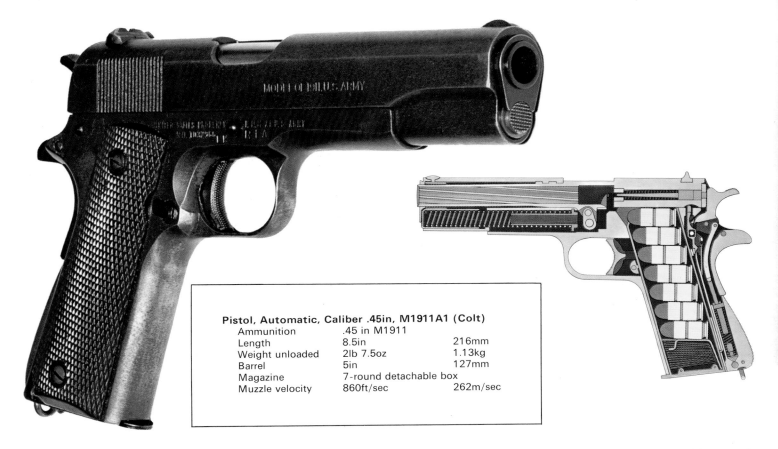

Pistol, Automatic, Caliber .45in, M1911A1 (Colt)

Ammunition	.45 in M1911	
Length	8.5in	216mm
Weight unloaded	2lb 7.5oz	1.13kg
Barrel	5in	127mm
Magazine	7-round detachable box	
Muzzle velocity	860ft/sec	262m/sec

The story of US military pistols in World War II is both short and straightforward, since it is almost entirely the story of the Colt Model 1911A1 automatic pistol. The Colt was yet another of John Browning's designs. Its origins go back as far as 1892, when he was first experimenting with recoil operation for hand guns, but the final design was not approved by the US Army until 29 March 1911, and manufacture was put in the hands of the Colt Company. During World War I the Colt was used by both officers and NCOs and as many other troops as could get hold of them, though there were by no means enough to go round, and at the Armistice the total quantities on hand in ordnance ledgers was less than 500,000. However, production continued throughout the inter-war years at a reduced rate and Colt had a production line ready to expand when war was declared again in 1941.

The Colt pistol was a remarkable weapon, for it was quite simple in its design, relying on the barrel and slide remaining locked together as they recoiled, and unlocking them by a swinging link when the pressure has dropped to a safe level in the chamber. There were only three main parts, the frame, slide and barrel, and the success of the weapon stemmed from its utterly straightforward and strong design. If the parts were assembled incorrectly the pistol would not work, and while this may sound obvious, it was not so with certain other pistols. Next, the construction was enormously strong

and safe. For instance, the slide could not be blown off backwards if ammunition of greater power was fired, and this could happen in some other designs; the trigger mechanism was safe and would only fire if the grip safety was squeezed and the trigger pulled. Finally, the trigger was actually disconnected from the hammer until the breech was fully locked.

The Colt fired the large .45in (11.4mm) ACP cartridge, which threw a 230-grain bullet at 860ft/sec (260m/sec) and made it one of the most powerful military pistols to have been in service during the war. The impact of the heavy bullet was quite enough to put any man out of action straight away, though the kick of discharge was considerable and it took much practice to be more than an average shot with it. However, it was in fact a most accurate pistol and once mastered it had an effective range of at least 100m, with plenty of velocity left to carry the bullet on beyond that and do a great deal of damage. It was in every way pocket artillery, though one needed a big pocket to carry it.

The US Army issued the Colt to all officers and NCOs together with drivers, signallers, machine gunners, mortarmen, and anyone who could make out a good enough case to get one. It is still in service as the standard side-arm of the US forces, and it is still the most powerful pistol in military use in the world – a remarkable tribute to John Browning.

But not all pistols were Colt automatics; there were not

Smith & Wesson 1917

Ammunition	.45 in M1911	
Length	10.8in	274mm
Weight unloaded	2lb 4oz	1.02kg
Barrel	5.5in	140mm
Magazine	6-round cylinder	
Muzzle velocity	860ft/sec	262m/sec

enough to go round. The US Navy, for instance, had to be content with the .38in Smith & Wesson Military and Police revolver, which was a very good substitute and perfectly effective at most pistol ranges of action. Over a million of these revolvers had been made by 1944 and issued to either the US forces or to British units. They gained a reputation for accuracy and pleasant handling that few others were able to equal.

Another revolver which saw war service was the Model 1917 Smith & Wesson, calibre .45in, of which large stocks

Top: His Colt M1911 pistol at the ready, a marine searches for Japanese in the jungle on Saipan in July 1944.

remained after World War I. It was a standard six-shooter with a solid frame and swing-out cylinder, and it had a good reputation and immunity to jams. Many were sent to Britain to arm the Home Guard, but about 100,000 were issued to both the US Marine Corps and the US Army. The military police were almost all armed with this revolver, as there were never enough automatics for them. When it was mooted that the Smith & Wesson should be scrapped in 1945, the then Provost Marshal General protested and insisted that sufficient should be kept to arm the police in any emergency. He had more foresight than many others, for Korea was only five years away.

All these pistols went through their service lives with scarcely any modifications from the original design. The Colt Automatic underwent minor changes in 1921, making the nomenclature the M 1911A1; the revolvers were hardly touched, and all the factories had to do was to turn them out in sufficient numbers to satisfy the demand. The introduction of the M1 carbine reduced the need for pistols to a more manageable level after 1942, but at all times there were plenty of side-arms in any US unit, whether authorized or not, and their users were fairly skilled in handling them.

Hand-Operated Rifles

Although the United States was the first belligerent nation of World War II to arm its troops with a self-loading rifle, it nevertheless had to use a bolt-action one as well, and this was the Springfield. The Springfield was an old design before the war ever started. It owed its origins to the Spanish-American War of 1898, where the American soldiers were impressed by the Spanish Mausers and somewhat disenchanted by their own Krag-Jorgensens. In particular, the Mausers were able to keep up a continual rapid fire because they were clip-loaded, whereas the Krags reloaded with single rounds into their magazines. In 1900 the US Army Ordnance Board set about developing a new rifle using the Mauser bolt and loading system. By 1903 they had a suitable model which incorporated some features from rifles other than the Mauser, and which also used a rimless round, since the Ordnance Board fully realized the difficulties of loading rimmed ammunition. In fact, it is worth quoting their words

on the subject: 'The Board is of the opinion that if a clip gun is to be adopted it should be designed for a cannelured cartridge. Rim cartridges do not carry as well in the clips as do the cannelured cartridges, and they do not strip as easily from the clip into the gun. There is also considerable difficulty

in getting the magazine so adjusted that the rim of the top cartridge cannot get behind the head of the one next below. When this happens the two cartridges are carried forward together when the bolt is closed, causing a jam.' This is an admirably succinct description of the curse of rimmed ammunition.

This 1903 rifle was destined to survive until 1945, and it was a fairly typical example of early twentieth-century weapon design, although its parentage owed nothing to one particular national designer or factory. Thus, while the locking system was on exactly the same principle as the 1898 Mauser, it was varied to make minor improvements. The cocking piece came from the Krag-Jorgensen, the

Springfield M1903		
Ammunition	.30in M1903 and M1906	
Length	43.2in	1097mm
Weight unloaded	8lb 11oz	3.94kg
Barrel	24in	610mm
Magazine	5-round integral box	
Muzzle velocity	2800ft/sec	853m/sec

Above: A US sniper in Burma with an M330c telescope fitted to his Springfield M1903 A4 bolt-action rifle.

magazine cut-off from the Lee-Enfield, and the two-piece firing pin was a US invention. In 1906 the design was re-chambered for a .30in (7.62mm) 1906 pattern pointed (spitzer) bullet, now known the world over as the 30–06. Not surprisingly the 1903 Springfield resembles the many Mausers of the same period, especially the 1898 versions. It has the same distinctive upswept handguard running back to the backsight, the same finger-channel in the lower fore-stock, the same length of muzzle projecting from the fore-stock and hooded foresight, the same sunken magazine with a flush bottom-plate, and the same slightly awkward straight bolt-handle.

The first models gained a reputation for extreme accuracy, based to a large extent on a complicated and beautifully made backsight which was ideal for target ranges, but not really practical in war. However, war did not come until 1917, and the design remained unchanged. By 1940 over 1,700,000 Springfields, M 1903 Pattern, had been made, and the large majority of them must still have been in existence, mostly in US armouries. About 1,300,000 of these had been turned out in the Springfield armoury alone up to 1939, when production stopped; the remainder were made in Rock Island. Springfield made no more because the factory turned over to the

Garand, and Remington took up a contract in November 1941 – a bit late, perhaps! But in fact Remington had had a fair start before this date as they had been funded by the British Purchasing Commission to make rifles early in 1941, and had spent the summer transferring the machinery from Rock Island to their factory in New York State. None of the rifles ever reached Britain, as the US took all the output, but it is an interesting example of the way in which some US industry was put on a war footing by British money.

When Remington did start producing, they simplified the rifle as far as possible to use stampings instead of machining. The backsight was reduced to a simple aperture, apparently without any loss of accuracy – indeed probably a gain – and the rifling was reduced to two grooves. This was a bold move at that time, but it made not the slightest detectable difference to the rifle's shooting. Woodwork was trimmed of all unnecessary frills, including the finger-grooves, and the general appearance was more 'utility'. It was still an excellent rifle.

When the last rifle was made on 23 February 1944, Remington had turned out 1,084,371. Included in that million was the Model 1903A4, a sniping version in which the components were, as usual, carefully selected, and the only sight was a fixed telescope. But the phenomenal output of Remington was scarcely enough, and late in 1942 the Smith-Corona typewriter company took on a contract for Springfields; they made almost a quarter of a million by 1944. The total made altogether during World War II was 1,318,951, making a grand total for all production since 1903 of 3,023,730, a large proportion of which must have survived the war and must still be in existence somewhere. After 1945 the rifle was only retained for sniping, at which it excelled, and it last served in action in Korea with US forces.

The British used the Springfield also, though only in small numbers. These were a rush quantity bought from reserve stocks after Dunkirk, and intended to make up the crippling loss of 90,000 rifles left behind in France. It was fortunate for the US Army that the entire British deficiency was not made up from Springfields, since when the US entered the war in 1941 less than half the army units had the Garand. The Springfield was continued in service as an infantry rifle until 1943. At first the US Marines were entirely armed with it, and the first infantry actions against the Japanese in the Philippines were conducted with Springfields. As the war progressed and the output of Garands improved, more and more Springfields were made available to Allied forces. Many came across the Atlantic to equip British and Free French troops, though only as a reserve weapon in the UK since the 30–06 ammunition had to be imported also.

There was one other bolt-action rifle in US service, though it was only used for training. This was the Model 1917 or 'Enfield', which was originally a British design before World War I. It had been intended as a replacement for the Lee-Enfield, which had attracted much adverse criticism when it first appeared, but the project never got anywhere until 1914, when the US was given a contract to make it in .303in calibre. Several thousand were made and known as the Pattern 1914, or P 14, and now are collectors' pieces. But the US Army was short of rifles in 1917 also and found it convenient to make the weapon in 30–06 calibre, turning out over two million before closing the line in 1919. In 1940 over a million were sent to the UK to equip the Home Guard, and the remainder went to US training depots. It is almost certain that none of these rifles ever saw combat use, but they filled a desperate need at a critical time, and without them the Home Guard would have been carrying shotguns throughout the war.

Self-Loading Rifles

The US Army has the distinction of being the first to adopt a self-loading rifle as a standard arm. There had been several attempts in other countries to produce self-loaders from the early years of the century, but it was not until the M1 Garand

first came into the hands of American soldiers in 1937 that any had been sufficiently successful to merit replacing the reliable bolt-action models. The background to the Garand is worth telling – it is only marginally applicable to this book, but it illustrates the care and determination that went into its development.

The first efforts to find a satisfactory self-loader started as far back as 1916, but it was not until 1931 that the US Army Ordnance Board felt that a suitable standard had been reached. At this point there were two contenders, a toggle-action rifle by Pedersen (who incidentally tried to get Vickers interested in the UK), and a turning-bolt action developed by John Garand. Both used a .276in (7mm) cartridge developed by the Frankfort arsenal, and the Garand design carried 10 of these rounds in its magazine. At the same time Garand tried his rifle in .30in calibre, since he realized that the US had large stocks of this ammunition, and it was as well that he did – for when the army chief of staff, Douglas MacArthur, was asked to approve the decision to adopt the Garand in .276 calibre, he flatly refused to do so and insisted that it fire the .30. Garand could demonstrate that his rifle was perfectly effective in this calibre, and so its acceptance was confirmed. Not for the first time, and

maybe not for the last either, existing ammunition stocks dictated the choice of a new rifle.

The outcome of this selection was that the magazine now held eight rounds, since the .30 was larger in all dimensions than the .276, but all other features were the same. The Garand was a conventional gas-operated rifle with its gas cylinder beneath the barrel, running right up to the muzzle. In fact the gas port was directly underneath the foresight, giving the rifle the distinctive appearance of having two barrels. The piston rod was therefore longer than with almost any other rifle, and it had the return spring acting on it, so that the bolt was actually pulled forward on the forward stroke, rather than pushed as with most designs. The mechanism was both simple and robust: the operating rod, which was an extension of the piston rod, bent round underneath the barrel and came up alongside the right of the bolt, where it ended in a cam slot engaging a small lug on the

Right: Marines armed with an M1 carbine and Garand M1 rifle prepare to hold off Japanese snipers on Iwo Jima during the conquest of the island in March 1945.

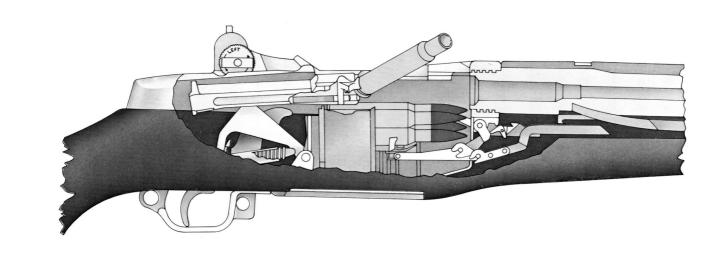

Rifle, Caliber .30in, M1 (Garand)		
Ammunition	.30in M1906	
Length	43.5in	1103mm
Weight unloaded	9lb 8oz	4.37kg
Barrel	24in	610mm
Magazine	8-round integral box	
Muzzle velocity	2800ft/sec	853m/sec

bolt itself and a cocking handle. The forward and backward movement of the rod first of all rotated the bolt to unlock it, then carried it back to extract the empty case, then pulled it forward to load the next round, and finally rotated it to lock again. The entire operation was performed in the open, without protection from the elements, yet it rarely jammed.

The whole construction was quite massive in comparison with other designs, yet it was no heavier. The body or receiver was enormously strong but quite short, since it had no need to house the return spring, and the backsight was mounted on top of it. The unusual quantity of ammunition

World War II. There were many attempts to copy it. The Japanese simply built identical copies, chambered for their 7.7mm round. In Italy the Beretta factory built M1s under licence for NATO countries and derived a version for the Italian Army which still survives in 7.62mm NATO calibre. Of all the stories of small arms, that of the M1 Garand rifle is one of outstanding success and satisfaction.

Another American success story is that of the little .30 M1 carbine, a most delightful weapon, though not as lethal as most of its users would have believed. This carbine arose from a sensible realization after World War I that pistols

carried in the magazine partly stemmed from a firm refusal on the part of the US Army to have a rifle with a projecting magazine; for some reason it was thought that this restricted the rifleman's handling and that it allowed dirt to enter. The eight rounds were carried and loaded in a charger which stayed in until the last round had been fed, when two things happened: first the bolt was held open by a catch, then the empty charger was shot out upwards, accompanied by a distinctive 'pinging' sound. It has been said that sharp-eared Japanese listened for this sound in jungle fights and charged when they heard it, as it meant that there was a short delay while the rifle was reloaded. It sounds good, but it probably never happened more than once.

The Springfield armoury made the majority of Garands, but by the end of 1938 only 7,500 had been issued, and in early 1941 the Winchester Repeating Arms Company was building them as well. By December 1941 both factories were in full mass-production. Between them they made no less than 4,033,353, of which $3\frac{1}{2}$ million were from Springfield.

There were some minor changes and improvements during the war, but none that made any serious alterations to the design. It was modified to take a muzzle grenade-launcher, and selected versions were used for sniping, though the bolt-action Springfield was better for both these tasks. In 1944 there was a call for a shortened and lightened version for airborne use, but a satisfactory model never reached the troops because of the old trouble that simply shortening a barrel does not produce a useful carbine unless the cartridge is changed also. After the war the design continued to be modified until it culminated in the M14 rifle of 1958. Up to that time the M1 Garand remained the standard rifle of the US Army, and several other armies in NATO too, and it was used throughout the Korean War in the same form as in

Carbine M1

Ammunition	.30in M1 Carbine	
Length	35.65in	905mm
Weight unloaded	5lb 7oz	2.48kg
Barrel	18in	457mm
Magazine	15- or 30-round detachable box	
Muzzle velocity	1950ft/sec	593m/sec

were not particularly effective weapons of war, however good they might be in the Wild West. A rough specification was drawn up for a light shoulder-arm for the use of troops not actually fighting in the front line, i.e. gun crews, drivers and the increasing numbers of signallers. The idea hung fire until 1938, when it was turned down because of the shortage of money, but in 1940 the success of the German parachutists brought the need for protection in rear areas into sharp relief. A hurried specification was sent out to no less than 25 manufacturers, who replied with some predictably varied ideas. Winchester came late into the race because they were committed to fitting out their factory for the Garand, but their idea was a scaled-down Garand, and it won.

The ammunition for the carbine was derived from the Winchester 1905 .32in self-loading rifle, with a lighter bullet which limited its maximum effective range to 300m (perhaps less), but this was a substantial improvement on what could be expected from a partially trained man with a pistol, and it was worth the weight of 5.5lb (2.48kg). A magazine holding 15 rounds gave a useful reserve of firepower, and the general shape looked and felt good. The mechanism worked by a short-stroke piston, one of the first to succeed with that arrangement, and when fired the little carbine was a positive pleasure to hold, in contrast to the powerful kick from the then-current full-powered rifles. It caught on immediately and became the most popular weapon on the Allied side in

*Above: Paul E. Ison of the First Marine Division
charges forward on Iwo Jima, carrying his
Garand M1 rifle.*

the whole war. First used in action in North Africa in 1942, it was rapidly taken up by the airborne troops and as many others as could get their hands on one.

In the Burmese jungle the carbine was invaluable, and it is still being used there today. In the Pacific theatre it was issued in very large numbers to the US Marines and all amphibious troops, who found it the best weapon for the often confused short-range fighting on the shores of the Japanese-held islands. Later on in the war a full automatic switch was fitted, together with a 30-round magazine, but neither saw action. Most users had a canvas pouch strapped to the butt with two spare full magazines in it, and it was accepted that the reduced power of the bullet would normally be compensated for by discharging more rounds. A folding-butt version was made for parachuting, though the short length of the weapon hardly justified it, and very late in the war a small number were fitted with an infra-red night sight.

Winchester and the inland division of General Motors made the majority of the 6,000,000 carbines produced up to 1945, and production ceased then, though it has been renewed since. In Korea the carbine was everywhere, as it was in the two decades of fighting in Indo-China and the Malaysian Peninsula. It has recently been bought for use by the Royal

Ulster Constabulary in Northern Ireland and will continue to appear for many years yet, for it seems to be as enduring and useful as the jeep.

Finally we have to record one other self-loading rifle that the US forces used, though only briefly. This is the Johnson, a brilliant but unconventional design using short recoil to operate the mechanism. Melvin Johnson tried to get the US Army interested in his rifle before the war, but having selected the Garand the army was not interested. The marines played with it, but the only serious order was from the Dutch East Indies, which requested 50,000 in 1940. The first deliveries coincided with the Japanese invasion, so the US Marines took the rest for their rapidly expanding units. The OSS organization took a few more, and it was found that because the barrel could be easily removed it was a convenient rifle for parachutists. Small orders kept the factory going until 1944, but Ordnance Board approval was never forth-

Below: A marine, his M1 carbine at the ready, prepares to rush a belt of ammunition forward to a machine-gun position on Tarawa, 1944.

coming, and despite continuous improvements production ceased then with a total of about 70,000 having been made. Some of these were lost to the Japanese, and some others were carried by marines in the Solomon Islands campaign; most stayed in the USA in training depots. After the war Chile bought about 1,000 for police use and the US Marines released their wartime stock for private purchase, so there are far more of these rifles in circulation today than their production and service use actually justify.

Submachine Guns

The United States was the third country in the world to develop a submachine gun, though it only did so commercially. The US Army was not interested in submachine guns until the beginning of World War II. The original Thompson appeared in 1918 as a trench-fighting weapon; it was just too late to be adopted for that purpose and languished as a gangster's weapon and general 'rough-house' gun for the next 20 years except for a tiny number used by the US Navy in 1928. In 1940 the British Army decided that what it needed most of all was large numbers of 'Tommy Guns'. A substantial order was placed with the manufacturers, who promptly set about finding sub-contractors to help them out – they had no actual factory, but relied on leasing to others.

The 1928 Model Thompson submachine gun was a very well-made gun – perhaps too well made, for the intricate machining work required in the design was very expensive and the strong steel construction and large magazine made it unnecessarily heavy for the job it had to do. These first Thompsons were the model first made in 1921 with only minor deviations; in fact, many of them had the '1' of 1921 overstamped to '8' and little else. They were the classic 'Tommy Gun' of all the gangster films, with two sloping pistol grips serrated for fingers, a finned barrel, wooden stock, and most prominent of all, a round drum magazine just in front of the trigger guard. By 1939 probably no more

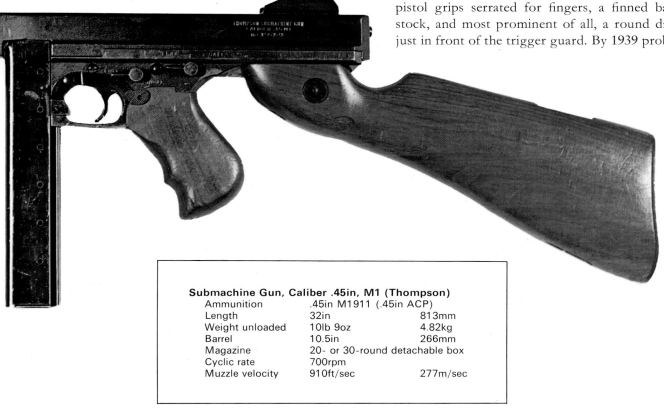

Submachine Gun, Caliber .45in, M1 (Thompson)

Ammunition	.45in M1911 (.45in ACP)	
Length	32in	813mm
Weight unloaded	10lb 9oz	4.82kg
Barrel	10.5in	266mm
Magazine	20- or 30-round detachable box	
Cyclic rate	700rpm	
Muzzle velocity	910ft/sec	277m/sec

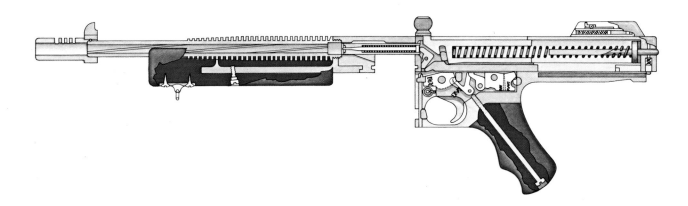

than 20,000 had been made of these striking but expensive weapons, and the company was almost in despair; the size of the new orders was a godsend to its sinking fortunes.

The Thompson was a novel gun in that it employed a form of retarded blowback operation which was unique. The arrangement used the friction of two inclined planes to hold the bolt closed for the time needed to let the bullet clear the muzzle, after which the usual blowback system applied. The drum magazine was another novelty, since there is no record of anything similar being used before, and it was presumably prompted by the need to carry a substantial amount of ammunition when dodging from traverse to traverse along a trench, not knowing what was round the next corner. The resulting gun was very much in the mould of its times, but as it was later clearly shown, a gun weighing 10lb 12oz (4.9kg) empty was too heavy by far for .45in pistol ammunition.

Nevertheless, with nothing else to buy in 1940, the British ordered 107,500 guns and the French added 6,000 which were later diverted to Britain. The US Army called for 20,450, and by August 1941 the combined orders, most of them from Britain, reached 318,900. The Savage Arms Company took the major share of the contracts, others going to a special factory set up by the Thompson patent holders. Eventually these two were turning out a total of 90,000 guns a month, and when the line finished in 1944 the grand total had reached 1,400,000. However, not all were the 1928 design. The US Army stepped in and simplified the design to make it easier to build and also easier to maintain. In March 1942 the M1 Thompson was type-classified, with a number of significant changes from the original.

In the M1 the blowback retarder was abandoned and the gun worked on the usual blowback principle. The drum magazine was replaced by a 30-round box and several features requiring machining were dropped. Shortly after this the complicated firing pin and hammer were replaced by a fixed pin on the face of the bolt. Even so, the Thompson was still taking too much factory effort and too few were being made. After prolonged and controversial trials at the Aberdeen Proving Ground in 1941 the US Army selected the M3 submachine gun and started to develop it in 1942. The M3 was in the best traditions of the vogue for simple, easily made weapons of the kind typified by the Sten and MP 40; it was made from sheet-steel stampings and pressings with a minimum of machining. There was nothing either unnecessary or beautiful on it; the lines were crude and practical, the mechanism elementary and the cost minimal. It worked, and could be turned out in large numbers, but the Thompson did not give in easily.

Despite all the obvious drawbacks attributable to the Thompson, it generated an extraordinary affection among those who used it. It may have been heavy, and it may have been awkward, but it had virtues which it retained throughout all the production modifications imposed on it: it was reliable and powerful. The .45in ACP round had plenty of punch, and the gun never stopped working no matter how bad the conditions. In Britain the commandos and parachutists who had been given Thompsons refused to give them up when Stens were offered in exchange. The same was true of those US units who were sufficiently independent to be able to ignore official edicts. So it was that the venerable gun of the Chicago gangsters was still being used in 1945 on all battle-fronts. It became such a legend in Ireland that one or two are still found in the hands of the IRA, though generally in these cases even the robustness of the Thompson has succumbed to neglect and ill-use.

The M3 was a worthy successor, had the troops realized it. For one thing it was all but immune to dirt, mud and water, since it had no openings in the body apart from the ejection opening, which had a spring flap. The bolt ran on two steel

rods which gave it a much smoother action and the cyclic rate was kept down to 400 rpm so that the gun could be held on a target without difficulty. In this it was better than the great majority of similar guns, including the Thompson, which all climbed upwards when firing automatic and could not be held down. An additional advantage was that with so slow a rate of fire there was no need to have a single-shot arrangement, since even the most ham-fisted shooter could pull off one shot and let the trigger go before firing another. But with all these points in its favour, the M3 was never popular in the US. The GIs called it the 'Grease Gun' or 'Cake Decorator', and its homely appearance and undeniably poor balance damned it.

In 1944 a further simplification was brought in: the bolt was now cocked by opening the ejection slot, putting the right forefinger into a hole in the bolt, and simply drawing it back! It worked well. Other modifications allowed the folding wire stock to be used as a dismantling tool, magazine loader and cleaning rod. No doubt it was better at these tasks than as a stock, for which it could scarcely have been worse since it slipped abominably in the shoulder and was poorly sloped for the average firer's sight line. The magazine was troublesome on all models, and its tendency to jam was never cured in the life of the gun. Nevertheless, it was a fine example of American inventiveness and ingenuity and it deserved a better reputation than it got.

Contrary to popular belief there was at least one other submachine gun in service with US forces during the war. This was the Reising, an unusual weapon that was designed in 1938 and sold to the US Marines in 1940. Readers will by now be familiar with the propensity of maritime forces to select their weapons and equipment in opposition to the army, and the US Marines have been past masters at this for generations – not always to their advantage, as the Reising showed. It was a fairly complicated gun with a mechanism that fired from a closed bolt – not the best way of arranging automatic fire – and it went further in its complication by not actually firing automatically at all in the usual sense, for it fired a rapid succession of single shots. To do this a hammer

was cocked for each shot, held back and then released – a quite different system from that employed with the usual simple bolt and fixed firing pin. To further complicate things the bolt was all but locked on firing, and the magazine, of which there were two sizes, was flimsy and liable to jam. The sum of these features was a hopelessly unreliable gun unless it was kept in tip-top condition and treated gently, and few soldiers can be expected to do that all the time. In its favour it can be said that it was light and pleasant to shoot, but this was not enough. Altogether about 100,000 of these guns were produced, and when the US Marines began to show a reluctance to accept more, attempts were made to sell the remainder to the Allies.

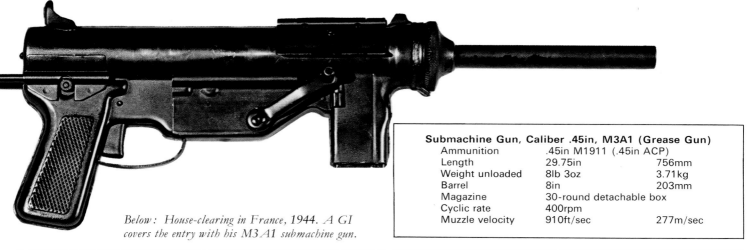

Below: House-clearing in France, 1944. A GI covers the entry with his M3A1 submachine gun.

Submachine Gun, Caliber .45in, M3A1 (Grease Gun)		
Ammunition	.45in M1911 (.45in ACP)	
Length	29.75in	756mm
Weight unloaded	8lb 3oz	3.71kg
Barrel	8in	203mm
Magazine	30-round detachable box	
Cyclic rate	400rpm	
Muzzle velocity	910ft/sec	277m/sec

Machine Guns

Unlike the British and the French, the Americans never developed a proper light machine gun after World War I. The reasoning for this is difficult to follow, but it seems to have come from a mixture of inexperience and financial stringency. The US Army was long enough in the trenches to appreciate the value of light machine guns, and they took over no less than 37,000 Chauchat guns from the French, with results that are still remembered in America – for the Chauchat was an unmitigated disaster. But it was not intended as a machine gun in the way that they are usually envisaged. The French Army had developed a theory of warfare that was entirely their own and they passed it on to the Americans, who were only too glad to pick up any tactical hints that they could. The idea was that infantry advancing across no man's land could protect themselves from the devastating effects of defensive machine-gun fire by firing back throughout the advance. The idea was, in other words, defence by attack, an extension of the already discredited theory of 'toujours l'attaque'. It was an idea that found a ready hearing among belligerent American generals.

The continuous fire was to be provided by men carrying the Chauchat, fired from the hip. The famous designer John Browning took up the idea, calling it 'Walking Fire', and produced his own gun for the purpose. This was a machine rifle, the Browning Automatic Rifle or BAR, and it saw a few weeks of action on the Western Front before the war ended. After the war it was adopted by a number of countries and became the standard squad-support weapon of the US infantry, so in 1941 the US Army took it to war for the second time. It was never a success, though it has always been highly regarded by its American users, perhaps more from national pride than any realistic appreciation of its virtues. The BAR is a classic example of the compromise that satisfies none of the requirements. As a light machine gun it was too light, and its 20-round magazine far too small – a fact that was recognized as early as 1918, when a 40-round box was produced, but this was for AA work only, as with this larger magazine the gun could not be easily fired from the bipod. As a rifle it was too heavy and offered little advantage over the Garand. Indeed, at one point late in the war the Aberdeen Proving Ground was asked to investigate the possibilities of giving the Garand a larger magazine and an automatic-fire capability, which would have meant the end of the BAR in the squad. It never happened, and the BAR continued in service until the end of the Korean War, still with the American attitude to it unchanged.

The war service of the BAR is quite impressive, as it was carried by US troops in all theatres and supplied in limited numbers to the British Home Guard in 1940. After the war large quantities of them were sold to friendly countries and saw action in most of the minor wars since 1945, including the Vietnam battles. In the USA various contractors produced over 350,000 BARs during World War II and Korea, but several more were also made by Fabrique Nationale in Belgium and Carl Gustavsfabrik in Sweden.

The US Marines, different as always in their weapon procurement, decided that the concept of a genuine light machine gun fitted in with their tactical doctrine. The only one which they could find in the late 1930s was the Johnson, a larger brother of the Johnson rifle which they had taken also. Undoubtedly the Johnson was an excellent weapon with many desirable features, and with more support from the US Army it could have been developed into a most effective gun. Long after the war it was produced in small numbers in Israel as the Dror, and was perfectly successful, though not good in desert conditions. For the US Marines it was apparently adequate though a little frail; however, it could be quickly and easily dismantled, which made it attractive for parachuting. At Quantico in 1941 a gun was carried by a parachutist, broken down in a weapon pouch, and 90 seconds after landing it was firing. About 10,000 were made and issued to marine units, the OSS and the US Army

Below: A Browning Automatic Rifle in the bow gives covering fire during a Pacific landing in 1943.

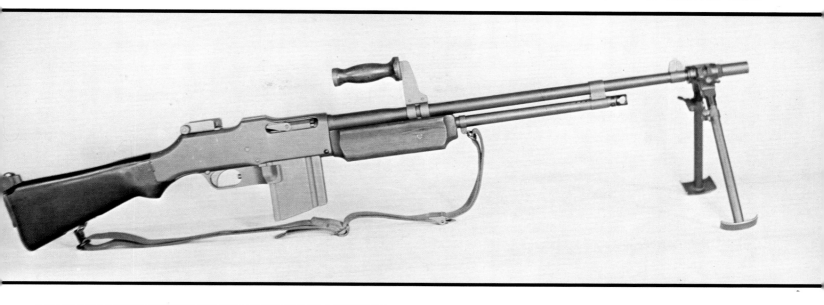

Browning Automatic Rifle (BAR)		
Ammunition	.30in M1906	
Length	48in	1219mm
Weight unloaded	16lb	7.28kg
Barrel	24in	610mm
Magazine	20-round detachable box	
Cyclic rate	500rpm	
Muzzle velocity	2650ft/sec	807m/sec

1st Special Force. The marines fought with it most successfully in the Pacific and continually pressed the army to let them standardize on it. The army always gave the same reply to these requests; 'The Marine Corps is a customer of the Ordnance Corps in small-arms matters, and consequently is reluctant to adopt an automatic shoulder weapon which is not an Army standard', and despite steady improvement of the Johnson, the matter rested there.

The Johnson light machine gun used the same short-recoil system as the rifle, but fed from a 20-round box magazine on the left side of the body. It had the same loading feature as the rifle, in which extra rounds could be pushed into the magazine loading aperture on the right side. The firer could therefore keep topping up his magazine so that he had an instant reserve for an emergency, and the side-mounted magazine did not seem to hinder any firers. The US Army 1st Special Force claimed that 'pound for pound it was the most valuable armament the force possessed', but even this support could not get official recognition for the Johnson, and it disappeared from service in 1945.

To the US Army a machine gun was a Browning, and indeed there were virtually no others. Browning swept all before him in 1917 with his designs for both the BAR and for a water-cooled medium machine gun, and from then on they were supreme. The Browning medium gun was very much in the tradition of the Maxim type in its appearance, and in its general method of working, since it used recoil to operate the mechanism. But Browning had to avoid the Maxim patent on the toggle locking, so he devised a much simpler and easier system using a vertical locking piece which was cammed upwards to lock the barrel and breech block together, and pulled down out of engagement as the system recoiled back. The barrel was water-cooled, the body was large and square, and the whole gun was mounted on a tripod. The performance using the 30–06 cartridge was very similar to the Maxim variety, and the only obvious difference to the casual glance was that the firing handles had been replaced by a single pistol grip and trigger. The gun could use either a canvas belt or a metal-linked one, and it was employed for exactly the same tasks as the medium machine guns in other armies. It went to war in 1918 with great success, and in 1919 a cavalry version was made with a heavy air-cooled barrel. This was also put into tanks, and it was quickly found that air-cooling was very nearly as good as using water, with a marked reduction in overall weight. It was soon put into service in the infantry, too, to supplement the water-cooled versions, and when World War II started the two types were used side-by-side. As production in-

Left: An air-cooled Browning M1919A4 attached to an armoured unit covers a road in France, 1944.

creased the heavier water-cooled guns were either converted or phased out into reserve stocks, and by the end of the war practically every Browning in infantry use was using the air-cooled barrels.

An oddity of the general run of Brownings was the so-called light version, which was type-classified in February 1943. There had been steady pressure since the start of World War II to lighten the Browning still further, or to introduce a proper light machine gun, but the ordnance corps resisted, no doubt for good manufacturing reasons, and took some pushing to agree to the light version. When it appeared it was seen to be a most unfortunate compromise, reminiscent of the German Maxim Model 1915. The gun was lightened somewhat by fitting a new barrel bearing and certain parts of the body, putting a shoulder stock on the

Machine Gun, Caliber .30in, M1919A4 (Air-cooled Browning)

Ammunition	.30in M1906	
Length	41in	1041mm
Weight unloaded	31lb	14.05kg
Barrel	24in	610mm
Magazine	250-round fabric belt	
Cyclic rate	500rpm	
Muzzle velocity	2800ft/sec	853m/sec

back of the body and a bipod on the front of the barrel, fitting a small pistol grip for the right hand, and very little else. The US Ordnance Corps pursued a sensible and steady course through the trials and tribulations of World War II, but they nodded on this occasion. Not only did the guns not function properly because of lack of power in the recoil, but they were by no means either light or portable. At 32lb 8oz (14.94kg) empty weight, the gun was a clear 50% heavier than any contemporary light machine gun. Add to this a 250-round belt and the idea becomes ridiculous, and so it was found to be. Few were made and fewer were used in action.

Below: A jeep-mounted M2HB .50 Browning in France.

Bottom: Firing an M2HB Browning at Japanese positions on Guadalcanal in 1942.

The other Brownings were without doubt resounding successes. The simple mechanism was highly susceptible to tuning and adapted well to the requirements for high-speed aircraft gunnery. All British and US aircraft in World War II were armed with Browning fast-firing guns, the US mainly

using the larger .50in (12.7mm) which had been developed at the end of World War I. The .50 was meant to be a heavier support gun for infantry and a more effective AA gun than the .30 size, but it found its main use in tanks and aircraft. In almost every way it was a scaled-up .30, with an oil buffer to dampen the rear movement of the breech block and stronger trigger sears. The ammunition has an interesting history, since the original round developed by Winchester in 1918 was nowhere near powerful enough. In the end the German Mauser 12.7mm anti-tank rifle was taken as a pattern and the resulting Winchester ammunition is still an almost exact copy of the 1917 Mauser, itself designed in a few months of urgent work when the first tanks were sweeping across the German trenches.

The .50 Browning, like the others, was given a lighter air-cooled barrel in the 1920s, and it entered World War II in that form. It was used mainly on vehicles, and when the jeep appeared in late 1942 it was commonplace to place a .50 Browning on a pillar mounting in the middle of the floor. It was also carried in the weapons company of the battalion for general supporting-fire tasks. In this role it continued until the late 1950s, when it reverted back to tanks. One of its drawbacks for all except deliberate fire was the comparatively slow rate of fire. In the AA role this was especially noticeable, as the main requirement for AA is to put up a heavy cone of

Air-cooled Browning .30

Ammunition	.30in M1906	
Length	38.5in	978mm
Weight unloaded	32lb 10oz	14.97kg
Barrel	24in	610mm
Magazine	230-round fabric belt	
Cyclic rate	500rpm	
Muzzle velocity	2800ft/sec	853m/sec

Browning .50

Ammunition	.50in	
Length	65.1in	1653mm
Weight unloaded	84lb	38.22kg
Barrel	45in	1143mm
Magazine	110-round metal-link belt	
Cyclic rate	500rpm	
Muzzle velocity	2950ft/sec	898m/sec

fire in order to get a few hits on the target. The .50 Browning also played a large part in persuading the US Army that it did not need an anti-tank rifle, at a time when most of the European armies were steadily building them. It was decided that the Browning would be as effective as any rifle, and in view of the origins of the ammunition this seems a perfectly reasonable argument. In fact by the time the US entered the war the idea of anti-tank rifles was out of date. The Browning had little practice in specifically defeating tanks, though it made an enviable reputation for itself in destroying light armour and lorries, particularly in the desert and Italy.

In summary, the US policy towards machine guns in World War II was not particularly adventurous nor innovative. This author, at least, will always be sceptical of the lack of a suitable light machine gun and the ineffective efforts to find one, but the main idea behind the ordnance corps was that they had a few good designs; they capitalized on them and were not deflected by continual modifications and changes. It is a sound policy for any procurers of equipment; the pity of it is that so few stuck to it.

Glossary

Action The action of a rifle is usually taken to consist of the body and bolt together with the trigger mechanism. It is not generally applied to other weapons.

Angle of sight The angle between the line of sight and the horizontal.

Ballistics Exterior ballistics is the study of the motion of a projectile from the muzzle to the target. Interior ballistics is the study of the motion of the projectile inside the gun.

Ballistite A propellant which incorporates a mixture of nitrocellulose and nitroglycerine invented by Nobel in 1888.

Bayonet A short-edged weapon that can be fixed to the muzzle of a rifle and used in hand-to-hand fighting. It is generally a two-edged blade knife, clipped to the barrel extension and in a few cases permanently fixed to the weapon and hinged out of the way for carriage.

Blowback The simplest form of automatic action.

Bolt A device for closing the breech of the barrel.

Bore The interior of the barrel from breech to muzzle, sometimes used to denote calibre.

Calibre The diameter of the bore measured across the lands. The lands are the higher portions of the bore left between the rifling grooves.

Carbine A short rifle, originally meant for mounted troops and provided with the necessary slings and swivels for use on a horse.

Cartridge Any disposable container for a single load for a firearm.

Charge The amount of propellant contained in the cartridge case.

Charger A metal holder containing cartridges, generally five for the magazine of a rifle. One loading motion inserts all five cartridges and the charger is swept away as the bolt closes. A clip performs the same function, but technically a clip falls through the magazine and out through a hole beneath. In the USA a clip is the preferred term and denotes both types.

Cordite The first British smokeless propellant, made from nitrocellulose and nitroglycerine extruded in long cords.

Detonation An extremely fast and disruptive form of explosion brought about by initiating a detonation wave instead of burning.

Ejection The function of the operating cycle of a small arm in which the empty case is removed from the gun.

Elevation The angle which a barrel makes with the horizontal when raised at the muzzle. When the muzzle is pointed below the horizontal the angle is called depression.

Extraction The function of the operating cycle in which the empty case is withdrawn from the breech. There are two stages to extraction; primary, in which the case is unstuck from close contact with the chamber wall, and secondary, in which it is fully drawn out.

Feed The function of the operating cycle in which a round is loaded into the chamber from the magazine or belt.

Free travel The space that a bullet has to pass over when it leaves the cartridge case before it engages in the rifling.

Handguard The protection around the barrel just in front of the breech, where the left hand supports the weapon in firing.

Hangfire A cartridge which does not immediately go off when struck.

Headspace The distance between the front of the bolt when closed, and the face of the breech.

Lands The portions of the bore between the grooves of the rifling.

Lead The conical section of the bore between the chamber and the rifling. It is sometimes known as leed.

Percussion caps The initiating method of a modern cartridge. A separate cap, usually in copper, is placed in the centre of the base of the case and is initiated by being struck with the hammer. The flash ignites the propellant.

Pistol, self loading Also known as automatic pistol. Any pistol which uses the power of the propellant to re-load itself,

Recoil The backward motion of a weapon when a bullet is fired from it.

Revolver A firearm in which a series of barrels, or a cylinder containing a series of chambers, is rotated before a firing mechanism. It is generally taken to be a handgun with five or six chambers.

Stock The woodwork of a rifle or machine gun.

Tracer Ammunition in which a small quantity of a brightly burning composition is filled into the tail of the bullet.

Trajectory The curving flight of a bullet.

Vertex The highest point in a trajectory.

Yaw Any tilting or angular movement by the bullet in flight.

Bibliography

BARKER A. J., *British and American Infantry Weapons of World War II*, Arms & Armour Press, London, 1969.

BARKER A. J. & WALTER J., *Russian Infantry Weapons of World War II*, Arms & Armour Press, London, 1971.

BENUSSI G., *Armi Portatili, Artigliere e Semoventi del Regio Esercito Italiano 1900–1943*, Intergest, Milan, 1975.

CHINN G. M., *The Machine Gun* – 4 vols., Government Printing Office, Washington DC, 1951–4.

ELLIS C. & CHAMBERLAIN P., *Handbook on the British Army 1943*, Arms & Armour Press, London, 1976; Hippocrene Books, New York, 1976.

HOBART F. W. A., *A Pictorial History of the Submachine-gun*, Ian Allen, London, 1973.

HOGG I. V., *The Encyclopedia of Infantry Weapons of World War II*, Arms & Armour Press, London, 1977.

HOGG I. V., *German Pistols and Revolvers, 1871–1945*, Arms & Armour Press, London 1970; Galahad Books, New York, 1971.

HOGG I. V. & WEEKS J., *Military Small Arms of the Twentieth Century*, Arms & Armour Press, London, 1978; Digest Books, Northfield, Ill., 1972.

JOHNSON G. B. & LOCKHOVEN H. B., *International Armament*, – 2 vols., International Small Arms Publishers, Cologne, 1965.

McLEAN D. B., *German Infantry Weapons*, Normount Armament Co., Forest Grove, Oreg., 1968.

MUSGRAVE D. D. & NELSON T. B., *The World's Assault Rifles and Automatic Carbines*, T.B.N. Enterprises, Alexandria, Va., 1967.

NELSON T. B., *The World's Submachine-guns*, International Small Arms Publishers, Cologne, 1963.

REYNOLDS E. G. B., *The Lee-Enfield Rifle*, Herbert Jenkins, London, 1960.

SMITH W. H. B. & SMITH J., *The Book of Rifles*, The Stackpole Co., Harrisburg, Pa., 1972.

SMITH W. H. B. & SMITH J., *The W.H.B. Smith Classic Book of Pistols and Revolvers*, The Stackpole Co., Harrisburg, Pa., 1968.

SMITH W. H. B., *Small Arms of the World*, Arms & Armour Press, London, 1978; The Stackpole Co., Harrisburg, Pa., 1946.

US WAR DEPARTMENT, *Handbook on German Military Forces* – reprinted by The Military Press, 1970.

THE WAR OFFICE, *Textbook of Small Arms*, HMSO, London, 1929.

WEEKS J., *Infantry Weapons*, Pan Books, London, 1972; Ballantine Books, New York, 1971 – reprinted 1975.

WILSON R. K. & HOGG I. V., *Textbook of Automatic Pistols*, Arms & Armour Press, London, 1975; The Stackpole Co., Harrisburg, Pa., 1975.

Index